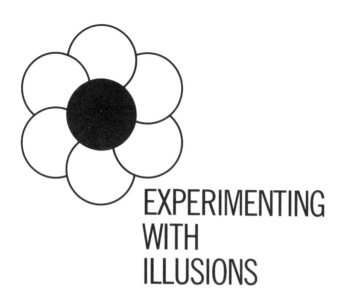

EXPERIMENTING
WITH
ILLUSIONS

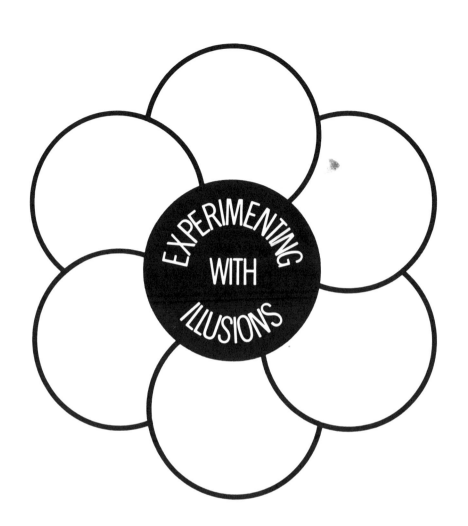

EXPERIMENTING WITH ILLUSIONS

BY ROBERT GARDNER

FRANKLIN WATTS 1990
NEW YORK LONDON TORONTO SYDNEY
A VENTURE BOOK

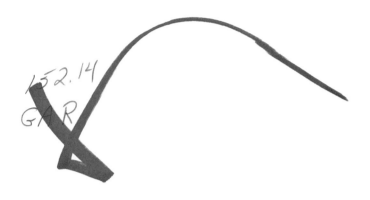

Illustrations by Vantage Art
Robert Gardner: pp. 39, 92, 93, 113; Museum of Modern
Art: p. 18; Scientific American: pp. 60, 62–64; Hartford
Courant: p. 87 (Paula Bronstein); Photo Researchers, Inc.:
p. 88 (Richard Weymouth Brooks).

Library of Congress Cataloging-in-Publication Data

Gardner, Robert, 1929–

Experimenting with illusions / by Robert Gardner.
p. cm.—(A Venture book)
Includes bibliographical references.
Summary: Explains how visual perceptions are processed
and suggests how illusions can be produced with images
and graphics.
ISBN 0–531–10909–7
1. Optical illusions—Juvenile literature.   2. Visual
perception—Juvenile literature.   [1. Optical illusions.
2. Visual perception.]   I. Title.
QP495.G37   1990
152.14′8—dc20   89–24780   CIP   AC

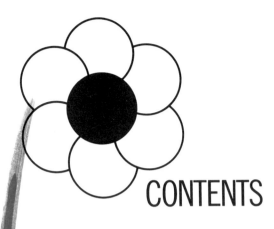

CONTENTS

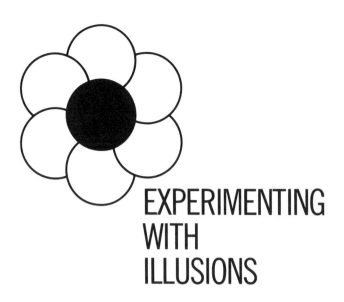

EXPERIMENTING WITH ILLUSIONS

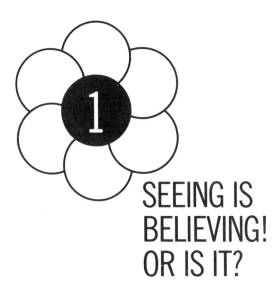

SEEING IS BELIEVING! OR IS IT?

Many people will tell you that "seeing is believing." But in this book you'll learn not always to trust your sense of sight or, for that matter, your sense of touch, temperature, hearing, taste, or smell.

We are aware of things around us because of our senses. We see a beautiful sunset; we hear thunder; we smell the roses in a garden; we taste a candy bar; we touch a soft, furry puppy; our hands, toes, and ears tingle from contact with the cold air of a winter day. But the perception of these events and objects that fill our surroundings depends on how our brain interprets them.

The signals that stimulate our senses are not what our brains perceive. The things we touch come in direct contact with the nerve cells they excite. The

9

things we taste are chemicals that touch the tongue where our taste receptors are located. Things we smell need not touch our noses, but the chemicals in these substances reach our noses in the form of gases. For instance, some of the liquid in an open bottle of perfume evaporates and moves through the air until it reaches our nose. There nerve cells sensitive to the chemical in the perfume are excited and send signals to the brain. But with both light and sound there is no direct contact between the object seen or heard and your eyes or ears.

Light does not have color. It is an electromagnetic wave—an oscillating electric and magnetic field that travels through space at 186,000 miles (300,000 kilometers) per second. When it strikes the sensory cells in the retinas of our eyes, it causes those cells to send impulses along nerve cells to the brain. Somehow the brain transforms those nerve impulses into the perceptions we "see." Similarly, thunder is heard only when there are ears to hear it. Sound waves generated by the sudden rush of air into the vacuum created by a lightning flash are the back-and-forth motion of air molecules. When these molecules strike our eardrum, they transfer the vibration to the middle and inner ear. Nerve impulses generated in the inner ear are carried to the brain, where they cause us to perceive something that we call sound.

Someone once said that if the connections between the ear and the brain and the eye and the brain were switched, we would hear lightning and see thunder. We have no evidence that any such thing has ever happened. However, we do know of people, called synesthetes, who are afflicted with a disorder in which some senses are "welded" together. For these people sound may have color, red objects may "burn" the hands with tiny "points," and the odor of flowers may "feel" smooth and cool.

THE MIND'S EYE • The world is perceived with brain cells, but everyone's brain is different. As a result, no two people perceive the world in the same way. Just ask several of your friends for their impressions about a person who is new to your neighborhood or school. Ask them separately so they are not influenced by anyone else. You'll see that the same person is perceived quite differently by different people.

Despite our different perceptions of the same world, there are a number of factors that seem common to all of us. For example, if you can hear two conversations, you can only concentrate on one at a time. You may pick up bits and pieces of each one, but you can't follow both simultaneously. Look at Figure 1. You may see a vase, or you may see the outline of two faces. One is called the

Figure 1: Do you see a dish or two faces looking at one another?

figure, the other the ground. Figure and ground will shift back and forth, but they can't both be the figure on which you fix your attention at the same time.

We tend to group together things that are similar and to separate things that are not. In Figure 2, for example, you can easily perceive the separation of the T's from the tipped T's, but the division between T's and backward L's is not as evident.

With only a glance to guide us, we generally can't grasp the number of things present if there are more than five. Given but a glimpse of some small words, you may

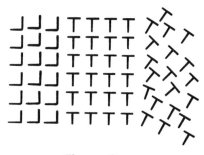

Figure 2

grasp two or three, but if you briefly see a phrase that is familiar, you may perceive as many as twenty letters. However, if presented a line of unrelated letters for the same brief time, you perceive only three or four.

We're very good at what is called closure. We automatically fill in spaces that we assume should be there. A circle with a gap in it may be perceived as complete. A long word with a letter missing, and various subjcets that are mispelled, will be read as if the letter were present or the letters in correct order. (Can you find such words in the sentence you just read?) A simple word may not be read twice if it appears at the end of one line and the beginning of the next. Here's an example:

PARIS IN THE
THE SPRING

You might like to design written passages that contain misspelled words and repeated words like the ones mentioned above. How many such words can you pack into a paragraph before the readers sense that something is wrong?

SIZE CONSTANCY • Look at a friend who is walking toward you. Does that person seem to grow taller as he or she approaches you? You probably don't sense any change in your friend's size. However, the size of the image of your friend on the retina of your eye doubles every time the distance between you and your friend halves.

To see that this is true, place a magnifying glass about 4 feet (1.2 m) from a bared glowing light bulb in an otherwise dark room. Place an index card beyond the magnifier and move it back and forth until you can see the image of the bulb clearly on the card. How large is the image? Now place the magnifier 8 feet (2.4 m) from the bulb and again measure the size of the image. What do you find? Can you predict how big the image will be when the magnifying glass is 12 feet (3.6 m) from the bulb?

The lens in your eye makes the same kind of image on the retina. You probably noticed that the image of the bulb was upside down. We have learned to see objects as if they were right side up even though the images they cast on our retinas are inverted.

Through experience you have learned that a smaller image on your eye means the object is more distant. It does not mean it is necessarily smaller. The people we see seem to have the same height whether they are close to us or far away. This is known as size constancy.

UPSIDE DOWN AND RIGHT SIDE UP • As we've said, the images of the objects we see are upside down on our retinas. If you were to look at an object that was inverted, its image on your retina would be right side up. Would you recognize the object?

Turn this book upside down and try to read the print. Can you do it? If you place a mirror perpendicular to the upside-down page can you read the print more easily? What's easier about it? What remains unchanged? Does a second mirror help?

Trace the outline of a map of the United States on a sheet of light cardboard. Use scissors to cut out the outline. Turn the outline upside down and ask a number of people if they can identify the object. Can anyone do it? Now turn it so that it is 90 degrees from the way it is normally seen in an atlas. Can anyone identify it now? How many know it's the outline of the United States when they see it the way it normally appears in maps?

Ask friends to identify upside-down photographs of people they know. Can they identify them? Cut out some newspaper or magazine photos of famous people. Paste them to sheets of cardboard. See if your friends can identify these people when they see the photos upside down.

Just for fun obtain several head-on photographs of famous people. Cut out two rectangular sections from each photo. One rectangle should include just the eyes, the other just the mouth. Carefully tape or paste these sections back onto the photos, but put them back in an upside-down position. Can your friends identify these people in upside-down photos? Can they identify them in right-side-up pictures in which the eyes and mouth are inverted?

FOOLING THE BRAIN • Though we are generally able to perceive the world in a way that allows us to live quite successfully, it is not difficult to get the brain to perceive the world falsely. In a classic experiment conducted nearly forty years ago, two balloons that could be inflated and deflated through valves connected to compressed air or to the atmosphere were placed about a foot (30 cm) apart in a dark room. The experimenters were able to illuminate the balloons from a concealed light in the ceiling. Subjects were asked to view the balloons with one eye from a distance of 10 feet (3 m) or more. When one balloon was inflated so it was bigger than the other, subjects would report that the balloon was moving toward them. Or if one balloon was made brighter, it would seem to move closer than the other balloon. If the balloons were inflated and deflated continuously, the subjects saw them move back and forth even with both eyes open.

In another experiment, two lines of light were viewed in an otherwise dark room. One line was longer than the other, but both were the same distance from the viewer. Subjects invariably perceived the longer line as nearer. If they were given a stick with a luminous tip that they could use to touch the lines, they soon learned that the two lines were the same distance away. After that, the lines were perceived correctly. Their view of this small segment of the world changed because of experience and learning.

In still another experiment, subjects looked through a small opening into a room. Though they did not know it, the room was distorted. Its floor sloped downward from the subject's right to his left. The left side of the rear wall was actually farther away than the right side. The windows on the wall were trapezoids with tapering sides that made them appear rectangular when set in the odd-shaped and receding walls. If two people of equal height stood in the room, the subject would see the farther one not as farther away, but as smaller, because the walls appeared to be parallel. Again, given a stick, the subject could not use it to touch things in the room. After some time and practice in touching things within the room, he would perceive that the room was distorted. Once he knew the true shape of the room, his perception of its shape changed and he realized why he had been fooled.

Such experiments help us to understand that perception is not certain or innate. We "see" things based on predictions that we make from past experience. In essence, we make the best bet we can based on what we have learned and the information that our senses provide.

Our ability to perceive the world seems to be learned. A young child who tries to touch the stars has not yet learned that such bright and seemingly near objects are far beyond her grasp. A blind person who suddenly gains her sight has to learn to see the world. At first, colors, sizes, and shapes convey nothing about the objects that possess these qualities. It requires time for these people to learn to use this newly acquired sense. In fact, they will often cover their eyes to avoid the confusion brought on by light and images.

Similarly, people from different cultures do not perceive the world as we do. If you show a picture of someone to certain African tribesmen, they may not see the face in the picture. When they do learn to see the face, they may look behind the photograph for the second eye of the person in the picture if it is not visible. The idea of displaying a three-dimensional world on a two-dimensional sheet is foreign to them. Many such people will not see depth in a picture. In fact, it was not until the fifteenth century that artists in our culture began to put perspective into their paintings.

ILLUSIONS VERSUS HALLUCINATIONS • Illusions, in a broad sense, are defined as any perception that doesn't agree with objective measurements or observations. They produce errors in perception that cause us to develop a false impression of the facts presented to our senses. Lines that are seen to be longer than they really are, straight lines that seem to be curved, colors seen that are not present, the appearance of depth in a two-dimensional picture, mirages, mirror images, a magician's tricks, and camouflage are all examples of illusions.

Artists use illusions to give us a sense of depth in the canvases they paint. They do this by using one object to partially hide another, by making one object smaller than another, by using bright colors to bring objects "out of the picture," and by using blue or gray to convey a haziness that we associate with distance. More recently, op artists have used striking visual illusions in their work. Notice the startling effects the lines in Figure 3 have on the eye.

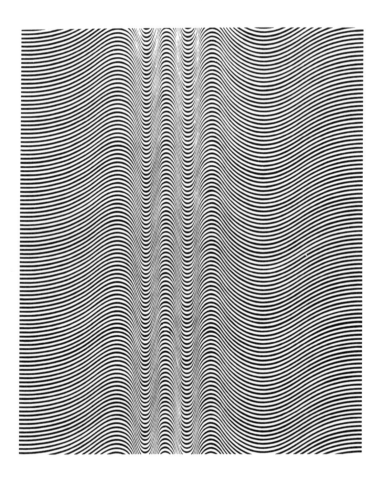

Figure 3

Architects use illusions to make things look natural. They may make the dimensions of a tall building larger at the top than at the bottom in order to erase the apparent tapering that arises from the decreasing size of the building's image cast on our retinas by the top of the building, which is farther from our eye. Magicians, of course, make extensive use of illusions to make us see things differently than they really are. And camouflage is used to prevent us from seeing things that really are present.

Hallucinations should not be confused with illusions. A hallucination is an object, figure, design, or some other mental image of which we are consciously aware but which does not arise from stimulation of the senses. Hallucinations are not caused by external stimuli acting on the sense organs. They seem to be induced by direct stimulation of the brain through some chemical or nervous mechanism. They may arise as a result of emotional stress, insulin, low blood sugar, epilepsy, high fever, psychoses, advanced syphilis, sensory deprivation, migraine headaches, and, most commonly, alcohol and other drugs.

The alcoholic who sees "pink elephants" or giant ants is hallucinating. The images that he or she perceives are real and frightening, but they are not to be found outside the alcoholic's mind. The hallucinations that accompany migraine headaches are generally mild and predictable. They usually consist of colorful squiggly designs that the person recognizes as a symptom of the disorder. But, again, there is no stimulus outside the brain that gives rise to these visual patterns.

The most common hallucination patterns are colored latticework designs, cobweblike lines, tunnels, cones, or funnels, spirals of various designs and colors, and past experiences that have been particularly emotional. The images are often brilliantly colored, symmetrical, and sometimes frightening.

In this book we'll concentrate on illusions. They're a lot safer and much more fun than hallucinations. Some of these illusions can be explained, others cannot. There are theories, of course, but no one can explain illusions with absolute certainty. There is much about illusions that we do not understand. The study of illusions, however, may lead to a better understanding not only of specific illusions but of the way in which a brain perceives the world around it.

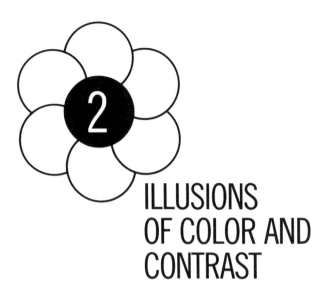

ILLUSIONS OF COLOR AND CONTRAST

We often design illusions of color and contrast for fun or to try to find out how we see and perceive things in the natural world. But there are a number of animals that use color and *lack of contrast* to hide from their enemies. For example, chameleons are able to change the color of their skins to match their surroundings. Hatchetfish have photopores on their skin that emit light. Though the fish have photopores all over their bodies, only those on the side opposite the source of illumination emit light. As a result, light from their photopores illuminates their own shadow. This makes it difficult for their predators, who rely on contrast between light and shadow, to track them.

A number of harmless moths and butterflies are colored like poisonous species. Birds that have learned to avoid the poisonous species will not eat the harmless ones, which, through evolution, have come to mimic the more dangerous animals. Inchworms, when disturbed, will clutch the branch on which they are crawling with their hind legs in order to project their bodies perpendicular to the branch. This makes them look like a twig of the tree.

These camouflage techniques, which are natural to animals, have been copied by man and used in wartime to hide airplanes, hangars, soldiers, and guns. The objects must be so colored and shaped that they match their surroundings when viewed from an airplane above as well as from the ground. Sometimes poorly camouflaged objects were detected by the shadows they cast. Their coverings might have matched the surroundings, but when viewed from a plane near sunrise or sunset, their long shadows revealed their true identity.

A RAINBOW BY YOUR SIDE • One of the most beautiful illusions in our natural world is the rainbow. It appears as a semicircle (or a part of one) in the sky when the sun shines through raindrops. If you have ever viewed a rainbow from an airplane, you know that it is really a circle. But on the ground we can see only half of it.

Light entering the raindrops is refracted (bent) and reflected back through the drops to your eye. You can easily see that light is bent when it passes from water to air. Simply put a spoon in a glass of water. Notice how the spoon appears to be broken at the point where it enters the water. Light coming from the spoon is bent when it leaves the water and enters the air.

To make a small rainbow you will need a large

"drop" of water. You can make such a drop by pouring water that has been boiled and then cooled, to remove bubbles of air, into a round-bottomed (Florence) flask. Find a large sheet of cardboard that is white on one side. In its center cut a circle with a diameter that matches the diameter of the spherical part of the flask. Support the flask with a clamp and place it in the center of a light beam from a slide projector. Place the cardboard between the projector and the flask with the white side toward the flask. Then move the cardboard back and forth, keeping the light beam on the water in the flask. You will find a place where you see a rainbow of light reflected from the water onto the white screen.

THE NEAR POINT • Your eye is your camera for viewing the world, but it is far superior to any manufactured camera. After light passes through the pupil in your eye, it enters the lens, which lies directly behind the pupil, as shown in Figure 4. The pupil is the small black hole that you can see in the center of your iris (the colored circle at the front of your eye). The lens bends light to form images on the retina. It is the retina that contains the nerve cells (rods and cones) that respond to light by sending impulses to the brain.

Although images are formed on our retinas, we do not see them there. Unless the nerve impulses generated in the rod and cone cells reach the brain we cannot see. But even when we do see things, we don't see them on the retina. They appear to be out in the space in front of us.

Your lens is able to bend light more or less by changing its shape. For objects close to the eye, the lens must be "fatter" in order to produce a clear image on the

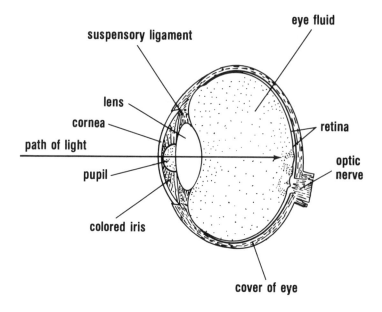

suspensory ligament

eye fluid

lens

cornea

retina

path of light

pupil

optic nerve

colored iris

cover of eye

Figure 4: Cross section of the eye.

retina. For distant objects, it must be thinner. Muscles around the eye control the suspensory ligament, which in turn controls the shape of the lens. As your eye muscles adjust to create a clear image on the retina, their degree of contraction subconsciously indicates to you the distance to the object you are viewing. If you keep moving an object closer to your eye, you will reach a point at which the object becomes fuzzy. You are no longer able to focus the light coming from it. Your lens simply can't get any fatter. This point is called the near point.

Hold this book in front of your eyes and move it toward your face until the print becomes fuzzy and you can no longer read it easily. Measure the distance from your nose to the book. **Be careful not to touch your eye.** Where is your near point?

THE CHEMISTRY OF SEEING • When light falls on the retina of your eye, nerve impulses are generated that carry messages to your brain. There are two types of light receptors in your retina. One set is cone-shaped and sensitive to colored light. These cells are located near the center of the retina directly behind the lens. The second set is rod-shaped and very sensitive to brightness but not to color. These cells are spread out over the sides of the retina.

In bright light you use your cone cells for vision. In dim light there is not enough energy to stimulate the cone cells. Consequently, at night you can see best with your rod cells. Rod cells are not found in the center of the retina. Therefore, to see at night you must use the sides of your eye. Rod cells contain a chemical called rhodopsin, commonly known as visual purple. The formation of this substance depends on the presence of vitamin A. The old story about eating carrots in order to see at night has some validity because carrots are a good source of vitamin A.

During the daytime there is very little rhodopsin in the rod cells because bright light bleaches the chemical into two smaller molecules. In dim light the concentration of rhodopsin increases. When you first enter a movie theater, it is very difficult to see even if you use the sides of your eyes. But as your pupils dilate and the concentration of visual purple increases, your eyes become much more sensitive to dim light as long as you use your rod cells. Cone cells probably contain pigments

too, but they are bleached so fast by light that the pigments have not been detected.

SEEING THE PURKINJE TREE • Because the pigments in the receptors of our eyes are bleached so quickly, an image will fade rapidly if it is fixed at one place on our retinas. This produces what is called an empty field. To avoid empty fields our eyes are seldom at rest. They constantly move in short jerky motions in order to keep the image from bleaching any one section of the retina. Normally, we don't see the treelike formation of blood vessels that lies in front of the retina. It casts a shadow on the retina, but the shadow is always in the same place so we don't see it.

If the shadow of this network of blood vessels, called the Purkinje tree, is made to fall on a different area of the retina, it will become visible. To make this happen, take a strong flashlight into a dark room that has a fairly large wall space. Shine the light at your eye from the side or below as you view the wall so that the shadow of the Purkinje tree will strike a different region of the retina. Move the light to and fro over a few millimeters. With a little patience, you should be able to see the Purkinje tree. The Purkinje tree may also appear during an eye examination.

TAKING PICTURES WITH YOUR EYES • To see how light can stimulate rod cells to create a picture on your retina, sit in a totally dark room for a period of at least 15 minutes. Then ask someone to lead you out of the dark room into a bright area. Keep your hands over your eyes as you make the transition because bright light coming through your eyelids can cause rhodopsin to break down.

Hold your head very still; think of it as a camera you are going to use to take a picture. Then remove your hands from your eyes for a moment. Focus your eyes on the scene before you, but don't move them. Concentrate on what you see. After not more than a second, close and cover your eyes again. What can you "see" now with your eyes covered? Are the colors the same as those you saw when your eyes were open? How long does this vision remain?

Are the colors you see using your visual-purple "film" affected by the colors in the scene you "photograph" with your eyes? Does the length of time you remain in darkness before taking your eye photograph affect the length of time you retain the photograph in your eyes and mind?

Ask other people to take a similar picture with their eyes. Do they "see" a similar picture? Do they see the same colors? Does a color-blind person see an image similar to the one you see? Does age or sex affect the nature of the picture seen with visual-purple film?

WHAT IS SEEING? • Researchers have reason to believe that visual signals coming from the eye are processed by three different systems in the brain. At one level are the signals that enable us to perceive the shapes of objects. At another level we perceive color, and at still another level we perceive motion and the spatial organization of objects around us. We are not aware of these three levels of processing. It's like watching a speaker's mouth and hearing his voice. We see it all as one action.

But, in fact, our eyes are watching the mouth while our ears respond to the sound waves. The only time we might be aware of the separate processing is when we watch a film in which the sound track is not in sync with the pictures. Then it is clear that the lips are not saying the words that we are hearing.

The processing of motion appears to be faster than the processing of color or shape. In a dense forest we may detect that something is moving without being able to determine its shape or color. To see shape we have to detect borders and colors, which seems to require more time than simply being aware that something is moving.

There is also evidence from victims of stroke (bleeding in the brain) that visual processing takes place at three levels. Sometimes these people develop selective types of blindness. For example, they may be able to see a face but not recognize it. They may be able to see shapes but only in black and white. Or they may be unable to see any shades of gray. The op-art effects that you saw in Figure 3 may be caused by the fact that they are strong stimuli for one processing system and not the others.

In 1953 Stephen Kuffler found that a light falling on a nerve cell in a cat's eye could have two effects. If the light fell directly on the cell, a burst of impulses was generated. But if the light fell on the region around the nerve cell it might shut off the impulses. And when the light was removed, the cell fired again for a short time. Other nerve cells were found that seemed to respond in the opposite way.

These "on-center, off-surround" nerve cells are believed to be responsible for something referred to as lateral inhibition. A response in one set of nerve cells may "turn off" nearby nerves in the brain as well as in the eye, ear, or other sense organ. Lateral inhibition may explain why we cease to smell the perfume in a room after a while. (Nerve cells near the odor receptors are stimulated and "turn off" the receptor cells.) Or why we stop hearing the hum of a refrigerator or a fluorescent light, but then, when it does go off, we are suddenly aware of the change. Perhaps lateral inhibition can also explain some illusions.

MACH BANDS • To see how the diminished stimulation of one section of the retina can increase the response of nearby receptors, you can experiment with Mach bands—bright and dark bands that surround shadows.

Place a fluorescent lamp about a foot (30 cm) above a sheet of white paper. Hold an opaque card an inch (2.5 cm) or less above the white paper. Notice the bright line, brighter than the white paper, just beyond the half-shadow.

You can do a similar experiment outside. Hold a white sheet of paper in sunlight. Let the shadow of your fingers fall on the paper. Move your hand far enough away so that there is a half-shadow around the dark shadow of a finger. Now look closely. You will see a band of bright white light, brighter than the white paper, just beyond the shadow. You will also see a dark band at the edge of the dark shadow. Can you explain these bright and dark bands?

SEEING COLOR • We perceive color. The light that comes to our eyes consists of electromagnetic waves. Sir

Isaac Newton, who was one of the first scientists to investigate color, wrote, "The Rays to speak properly are not colored. In them there is nothing else than a certain Power and Disposition to stir up a Sensation of this or that Colour."

Thomas Young first proposed a theory of color vision in the early 1800s. He suggested that there were three types of color receptors (cones). By stimulating these receptors with light of different wavelengths we perceive all the colors. As you will find later, mixing red and green light produces a color we call yellow. The reason for this, according to Young, was that an equal stimulation of red and green receptors produces the sensation of yellow in the brain. Similarly, red and blue produces magenta or purple, and green and blue gives rise to cyan. Equal stimulation of all three types of receptors produces white.

Later, Ewald Hering proposed a theory of opposing colors. He suggested that red and green are opposing colors because there is no reddish green. For the same reason blue and yellow are opposing colors. He also assumed that black and white were in opposition.

Present-day research indicates that there are three types of cones that respond to wavelengths that we perceive as red, blue, or green. However, before the signals from the cone cells are sent to the brain they are coded. The red and green signals are "weighed" as two-color difference signals before an impulse is generated. This signal, called a yellow signal, is then weighed against signals from the blue receptors before a final impulse is sent to the brain. So it seems that both Young and Hering were on the right path in their analyses of color vision.

Of course, most light is a mixture of various wavelengths. The comparison of wavelengths is made by nerve cells whose signal rate is increased by one kind of cone cell and decreased by signals from another kind.

About thirty years ago Edwin Land conducted some amazing experiments. His investigations showed that our ability to perceive color is more complicated than Young and Hering had thought. Land placed a variety of objects of different color on a table. He then took two black-and-white photographs of the objects. However, in taking one photo he placed a red filter in front of the camera. Before taking the second photo he placed a green filter in front of the camera. He made a transparency from each of these two black-and-white photographs. He then placed the transparencies in separate slide projectors and let the two images overlap on a screen. The transparency made from a photograph taken through red light was illuminated by red light. This was done by placing a red filter in front of the projector. Similarly, green light was used to illuminate the other image. What Land found to his amazement was that the black-and-white images now showed all the colors originally present in the scene he had photographed.

Further experimentation revealed that he could use a red filter to illuminate one image and white light to illuminate the other. The results were the same as before. All he, had to do was use a long wavelength to illuminate the photo taken through a red filter and a shorter wavelength to illuminate the other. In fact, he could use two different wavelengths of yellow light and obtain a colored image on the screen. Eventually, he found what he called a "balance point." The balance point was a yellow color. One image had to be illuminated with light that had a longer wavelength than the yellow and the other with light of a shorter wavelength. As long as the superimposed black-and-white images were illuminated with light that lay on either side of the balance point, many colors would appear.

Land's experiments suggest that the eye can provide the brain with all the information it needs to perceive all the colors as long as it receives colors from either side of the balance point. You might like to see if you can repeat Land's experiment. Or you can do the experiment "A Strangely Colored Shadow" on pages 35–37, which is a less ambitious modified version of Land's experiment.

MIXING COLORS • As Thomas Young and others found, all the visible colors can be made by mixing red, green, and blue light. You can test this for yourself by building a light box.

Figure 5 shows you how to make the light box. First, you will need a cardboard box about 1 foot (30 cm) on each side. The opening in the side opposite the bulb can be covered with a mask that has three 1-inch-wide (2.5 cm) slits cut in it. The mask can be made from black construction paper. Each slit should be covered with a small sheet of colored plastic material. These light filters can be obtained either from a scientific supply company, a company that supplies filters for theater lighting, or various other sources. If possible, these filters should allow only one color to pass through. To test them, hold two filters of different colors together like a sandwich. When you look through the two filters, you should not be able to see anything.

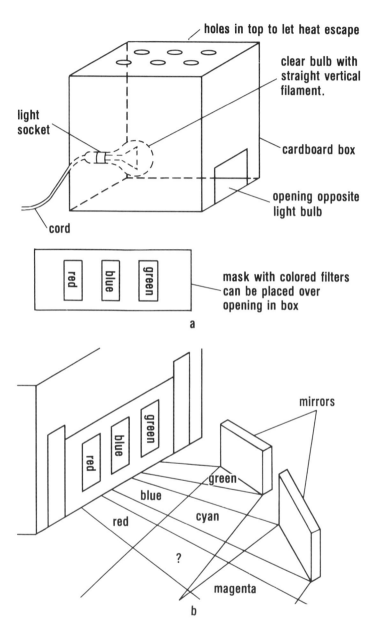

Figure 5: A light box.

Allow the beams of red, green, and blue light coming from the light box to fall on a white piece of paper. Using one or two mirrors you can mix the light by making the beams cross, as shown in Figure 5b. The color you get when you mix green and blue light is called cyan. Notice that you can vary the intensity of the color by changing the tilt of the mirror. When you mix red and blue you get magenta. What color do you get when you mix red and green light? Can you mix all three colors to obtain white?

COLORS IN COLORED LIGHT • Cut some small pieces from various colored sheets of construction paper. Make the pieces small enough to fit into the beams of colored light coming from your light box. In this experiment you'll be looking at colored objects in lights of different color. Remember that a red object looks red in ordinary white light because it reflects only red light. The other colors are absorbed. Can you explain why other objects are blue? Green? Yellow?

Be sure the room you are working in is very dark except for the colored light coming from your light box. Then lay a piece of red paper in the red light beam. What color does the red paper have in red light? What does it look like in blue light? In green light? What does a piece of blue paper look like in each of the colored beams? How about green paper? Yellow? Cyan? Magenta? White? Black?

Next time you are under a sodium-vapor street-lamp, look at various colored objects in its yellow light. Try to explain why different colored objects look as they do in different colored light.

COLORED SHADOWS • Colored shadows are all around us. Just look at the blue shadows cast on snow on a bright winter day or the rosy shadows seen at sunrise. Look for colored shadows on the wall and ceiling around a Christmas tree.

If you hold a pencil in white light, it will cast a black shadow. But what will it look like if various colored lights fall on the shadow? To find out, you can place a pencil upright on the blue beam coming from your light box. The pencil has a black shadow. Does it cast a black shadow when placed on the other two colored beams? But what happens when you use a mirror to reflect some red light onto a black shadow? When you reflect blue light onto a black shadow? Green light onto a black shadow? Can you make a yellow shadow? A cyan shadow? How about a magenta shadow?

Using mirrors to reflect the colored light, see if you can give a shadow colored bands like those shown in Figure 6. What other colored shadows can you make? How could you make large colored shadows at home or in school? Where else can you find colored shadows?

A STRANGELY COLORED SHADOW • Obtain two overhead projectors. (If you are unable to obtain such projectors, you can do a micro version of this experiment using flashlights, a small cylinder to cast shadows, and colored cellophane to cover one of the flashlights.) Cover the stage of each projector with a piece of cardboard that has a hole in its center. The hole should be about 4 inches (10 cm) in diameter. Cover one of the holes with a red light filter. Use the two projectors to cast shadows of your hand held in front of a white screen

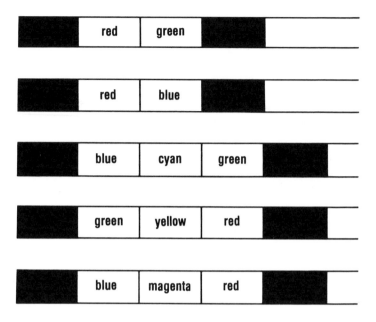

red	green		

red	blue		

blue	cyan	green	

green	yellow	red	

blue	magenta	red	

Figure 6: Colored Shadows.

or wall. How many shadows of your hand are there when both lights are on? One shadow is illuminated by red light. What color would you expect it to be? Were you right? You might expect the other shadow to be black since it is illuminated only by white light. But you'll notice that it is cyan, a combination of green and blue lights. Can you explain why? How is this experiment related to Land's experiment, which you read about earlier in this chapter?

Repeat the experiment using a blue filter instead of a red one. Can you predict what color each of the two shadows will be? What will you find if you use a green filter?

This experiment, known as Meyer's experiment, seems to be related to the colored shadows you've just seen. Place a small light gray square on a sheet of bright-red paper. Then lay a sheet of thin onion skin or toilet paper over the gray square and the bright paper. The gray square will take on a greenish tint. What do you think will happen if you repeat Meyer's experiment using a gray square on a bright-green paper? On a bright-blue paper?

COLOR ON COLOR: BACKGROUND EFFECTS • Cut some small equal-size squares from sheets of red, orange, green, cyan, and magenta construction paper. Paste one of each color onto a larger background square that is blue. Then repeat the process using yellow as the background. Which colors seem brighter on yellow? Which seem brighter on blue? Can you explain why the background has the effect it does? Do colors seem brighter when viewed with your head between your legs like a football center preparing to snap for a punt?

Now paste small squares of red, orange, yellow, green, and blue onto larger white and black squares. Do any of the colors look different on a black background than on white?

On a clear day when the sky is very blue, cut a hole in the center of a sheet of white cardboard or a stack of several sheets of white paper. Look at the blue sky through the hole in the white sheet while standing in the shade. What is the color of the sky? Repeat the experiment in sunlight with your *back* to the sun. (**Don't look at the sun!**) As you look through the hole to the sky, the sun behind you will illuminate the white paper. What is the color of the sky now? Why do you think the color changed?

Use colored marking pens to write on colored sheets of construction paper. Try black on yellow, red, green, blue, etc. Then try blue on different backgrounds. Repeat using red, green, yellow, and magenta pens on various colored backgrounds. Do some combinations stand out better than others? Can you get the same effect of depth as in those magazine ads where the colored letters appear to be floating above their background?

On a sheet of yellow paper make some small blue circles. The circles should be about one diameter apart. If you look at the sheet from a distance of 20 feet (6 m) or more, what do you see?

CONTRAST • You've seen that some colors stand out because of their contrast with the background. For example, black on yellow provides good contrast. But magenta on red may be barely visible. Black and white provide good contrast too, as you can see in the first photograph on page 39. The circle is uniformly gray. However, it's clear from the second photo that there is an illusion when you place a divider across the gray circle.

To see that it really is an illusion, make a copy of the design in the photographs. The circle is about a foot (30 cm) in diameter. Make two small holes in a 5″ × 8″ card so that you can place one hole over the gray on the black side and one over the gray on the white side. Without the background both grays appear the same, as you can see.

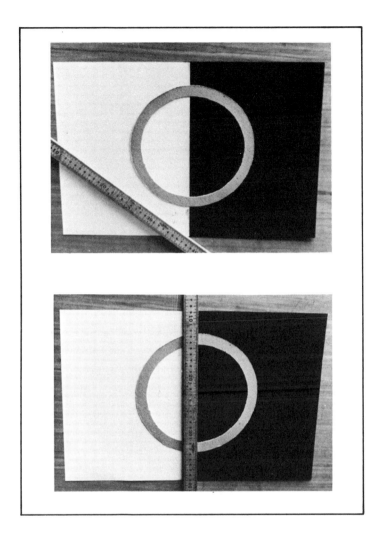

Top: A gray circle on a black-and-white background. *Bottom:* Notice the illusion on contrast when a divider is placed across the gray circle. By dragging the ruler to the right you can "pull" the darker gray into the black background.

Your brain seems to perceive brightness in a relative way. A light bulb that appears to be very bright in an otherwise dark room may go unnoticed if turned on at noon on a bright sunny day. When you place the stick across the gray circle, you immediately notice there are now two sides. We tend to fix our gaze on one side or the other, and the difference in contrast on the two sides of the circle becomes evident.

Here is one explanation for the illusion. (Maybe you can suggest another.) Involuntary jerky movements of your eyes cause light from the gray circle to fall on receptor cells that have just been stimulated by light from the bright white background. These cells are "tired" from sending impulses in response to all the white light. As a result, they do not send as many impulses as they normally would when gray light shines on them. The brain perceives this to mean a darker gray. On the other side, the black background sends very little light to the eyes. As a result, the receptor cells on that side are "refreshed" and can respond to the gray by sending more impulses than normal. The brain perceives this to mean that the gray is lighter than normal.

But now watch an even more amazing illusion. Slowly pull the dividing stick toward either side of the design. You will see the lighter or darker gray "dragged" into the other half of the design. Why do you think this happens?

You can make a similar design with a gray circle on red and blue in place of black and white. Or on blue and yellow. Are the effects similar? Can you still drag the gray?

Figure 7: Are these spots before my eyes?

SEEING SPOTS AT INTERSECTIONS, AND IRRADIA-TION • Figure 7 might represent the map of a city or a view through a window at night. But notice the spots at the intersections. Can this illusion be explained in the same way that the contrasting darkness of the gray circle was?

An effect that might be regarded as the opposite of what you have just seen is called irradiation. You can see this effect by holding a pen or pencil across the top of a bright light bulb. Notice how the bright light seems to make the pencil appear thinner than it actually is in the vicinity of the bright light. Or look at a new moon. The bright part of the crescent moon appears to have a larger radius than the darker outline of the rest of the moon. If you have a flashlight bulb, you can connect it to one, two, and three D-cells. Notice that as the filament grows brighter, it also seems to become broader. Could this be the result of the spread of light stimulation over a wider area of the retina? Or is it the result of the natural involuntary movements of the eye?

AFTER-IMAGES • Fix your gaze on a bright light for a couple of seconds, being careful not to move your eyes. Then close your eyes. What you see is a positive after-image. There is a bright light surrounded by a darker background—an approximate representation of what you saw. It is probably due to the continued stimulation of the retina. Some of the energy that entered the eye is still causing nerve impulses to be generated.

There are also negative after-images. Try staring at a bright-green card on a white sheet of paper for about 30 seconds. Notice the little pink fringe that develops around the card. This is due to those involuntary eye movements again. After you've stared at the green card, turn your eyes quickly to another sheet of white paper. You will see a pink or magenta card on the white background. This is a negative after-image. You see the complementary color of green (the combination of the parts of the spectrum other than green). It's similar to a photographic negative where the bright light causes a silver deposit that makes the film dark, while dimly lighted parts of the film remain clear. Can you predict what you'll see if you stare at a bright-red card and then look at its after-image? How about a blue card? A yellow card?

Try this when your eyes are rested. Shortly after awakening is a good time. Produce an after-image by staring at something bright (**not the sun!**). Then turn your eyes to a nearby white wall and then to a more distant white wall. What happens to the size of the after-image? Can you explain the change in size?

Cover one eye while staring at a bright light with the other eye. Can you see the after-image with both eyes or only with the one that was open? Using bright crayons, magic markers, or oil paints, make a design of a flag like the one shown in Figure 8. Starting with green at the top stripe, color the alternate stripes green and

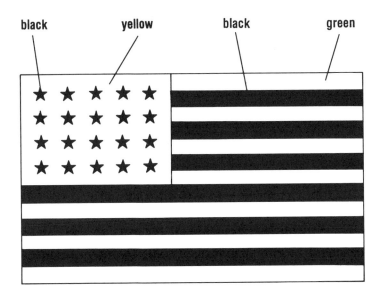

Figure 8: You can make your own flag after–image using this diagram as a guide.

black. Make the background for the stars yellow, and paint the stars themselves black. Can you predict what you'll see if you stare at the flag for half a minute and then look at the after-image? Design some patterns of your own for creating interesting after-images.

FOCAL LENGTH AND COLOR • Cover the opening in the light box you used before with a mask that has two narrow, vertical, parallel slits in it. Make the slits about 2 or 3 inches (5–8 cm) long and as narrow as possible, about $1/16$ of an inch or 1.5 mm. They should be about an inch (2.5 cm) apart. Two thin rays of light will emerge from the box. You can see them clearly if you place a white sheet of paper on the floor in front of the slits. Place a cylindrical plastic jar of water, about 2 or 3 inches (5 or 7.5 cm) in diameter, on the two narrow beams. Notice that the rays are brought together to a point. The jar of water represents the lens of your eye in two dimensions.

You can make red or blue rays by placing colored filters over the slits. Which rays, red or blue, are brought together closer to the "lens?" Suppose you are looking at a blue object. Your lens brings the blue rays spreading out from some point on the object to a point on your retina. You then look at a red object that is just as far away as the blue one. To bring the red rays together on your retina, will your eyes have to get fatter? Or will they have to get thinner?

As you learned earlier, we subconsciously determine the distance of objects by how much we have to fatten our lenses in order to see them. Remember the fatter lens is used to see near objects.

Based on what you have seen in this experiment, do you think a red object will appear closer or farther away than a blue object at the same distance? What can you do to test your prediction? On the basis of this experiment, why does it make sense to have the brake lights on cars covered with red glass?

RETINAL RIVALRY • If you cover one eye with a red filter and the other eye with a green filter, do you think you'll see everything as red, green, or yellow? Or do you expect to see something else? Try it. What do you find?

Try this experiment with other people. Are the results with everyone the same? Repeat the experiment using different combinations of colored filters. What do you find?

CHANGING COLORS • Look at the colors in a brightly colored painting. Then cover part of the picture with a card that has a small hole in the center so you can see only one color. Does the color that you see through the card appear to be different than when it is viewed in the presence of other colors? Can you explain why?

Look at some heavy black print on white paper. Now cover the print with a piece of black paper that has a hole in it. Does the print look darker or lighter when viewed through the black card?

"THE WORLD THROUGH ROSE-COLORED GLASSES" •
Look at a daylight scene through a yellow filter. Does it look "warmer" than usual? Does it look "cooler" through a blue filter? Why do you think the world looks different through colored filters?

COLOR FROM BLACK AND WHITE • If you hold the black-and-white design in Figure 9 close to your eyes, you will see color between the black lines. Could this be related somehow to Edwin Land's experiments?

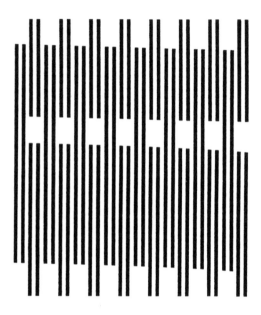

Figure 9: Color from black and white.

Try spinning an enlarged copy of the circular patterns shown in Figure 10. You can fasten the design to a circular sheet of cardboard. Then put it on a record turntable, spin it on a pin, or fasten it to the shaft of a small electric motor. When the design is spinning you can see color between the lines. Is the color you see

Figure 10: Color from spinning
black and white lines.

related to how fast the design is turning? Do different people see different colors? If you replace the black and white with red and blue or green and red, what colors will you see when the design is spinning?

RED AND BLUE AT TWILIGHT • Paste a bright-red design and a blue or cyan design onto a sheet of black paper. Take the paper outside or place it near a window after the sun sets and twilight turns slowly to night. Which color disappears first in the dim light? What does this tell you about the eye's sensitivity to different colors?

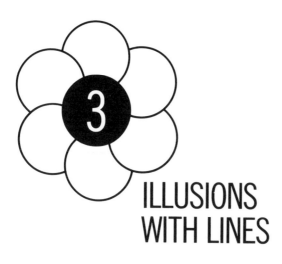

ILLUSIONS
WITH LINES

Some of the simplest illusions are made from straight lines. If you can draw a straight line with a ruler, you can easily draw many of the illusions you'll find in this chapter.

VERTICAL VERSUS HORIZONTAL ILLU-SIONS • Ask someone to draw a horizontal line on a piece of paper or a blackboard. Then ask that person to draw a vertical line that is equal in length to the horizontal line. It can be drawn from either the center or the end of the horizontal line. You will find that the vertical line drawn is almost always shorter than the horizontal line.

Look at the inverted T in Figure 11. Do you think the vertical or horizontal line is longer? Now measure them. What

Figure 11: Which line appears to be longer?

do you find? Vertical objects always look longer than horizontal objects of the same length. A tree looks much taller when it is standing than after it is cut down. Why should vertical objects appear longer than horizontal ones of equal length?

Some people believe it is because it requires more work to move our eyes vertically than to move them the same distance horizontally. What do you think? Figure 12 contains a number of similar illusions having to do with the apparent difference in equal distances.

THE NECKER CUBE • A rather well-known illusion is the Necker cube, shown in Figure 13. If you stare at this drawing for a few seconds, you will find that the shaded side of the "cube" will shift from being on the apparent front side of the cube to the rear. You see the orientation of the cube change. Sometimes blinking will help you to see the alternate views. Our brain can't decide which is the real orientation because either one is a logical way to view the drawing. Would we make the same mistake if we looked at a real three-dimensional cube?

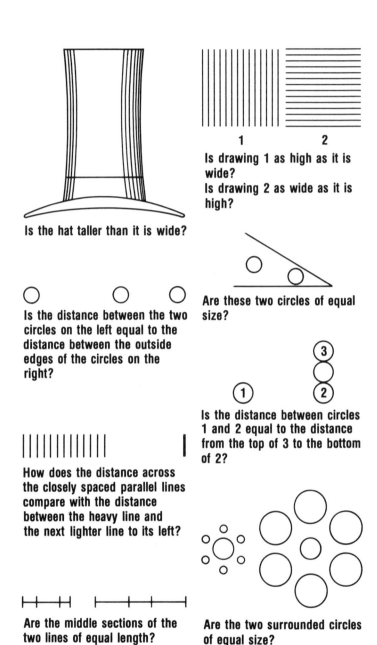

Is the hat taller than it is wide?

Is drawing 1 as high as it is wide?
Is drawing 2 as wide as it is high?

Is the distance between the two circles on the left equal to the distance between the outside edges of the circles on the right?

Are these two circles of equal size?

Is the distance between circles 1 and 2 equal to the distance from the top of 3 to the bottom of 2?

How does the distance across the closely spaced parallel lines compare with the distance between the heavy line and the next lighter line to its left?

Are the middle sections of the two lines of equal length?

Are the two surrounded circles of equal size?

Figure 12: Equal lengths.

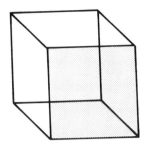

Figure 13: Necker's cube.

Here's a way to make a Necker cube that leads to a sudden change in perception. Carefully draw a hexagon. Then draw diagonals connecting the opposite corners. Stare at the midpoint. What have you drawn? Do you perceive it differently as you stare for some time?

An experiment was performed to find out whether this illusion was due to the eye or the brain. It's one that you can try too if you have a camera with a flash attachment. A Necker cube was drawn in heavy lines and placed in a room in front of a subject. The room was darkened and the subject's eyes were allowed to become dark-adapted for about 20 minutes. The drawing was then illuminated by means of a flash from a camera. After the flash, the subject saw the cube as an after-image. Even as an after-image the front of the cube can become the rear. The ambiguity (two interpretations) of the figure still exists. Since the after-image is the result of an image that is fixed on the retina, the ambiguous effect must arise in the brain. Some other ambiguous figures are shown in Figure 14. Like most such illusions, you can't perceive both meanings at the same time.

Look at this drawing. You will see a profile of an old woman or a view of a young woman. The young woman's chin is the old woman's nose. It was first drawn by W. E. Hill, a cartoonist, in 1915.

You can see this figure as either a rabbit looking to the right or a duck looking to the left.

Figure 14: Other ambiguous figures.

SOME FAMOUS LINE ILLUSIONS: WHERE LINES IN-TERACT • In Figure 15 you can see a number of illusions made by the scientists for whom they are named.

In the Ponzo illusion the upper horizontal line appears to be longer. Is it really longer? You can produce a similar illusion by placing two small squares of equal size on a photograph of railroad tracks that seem to converge in the distance.

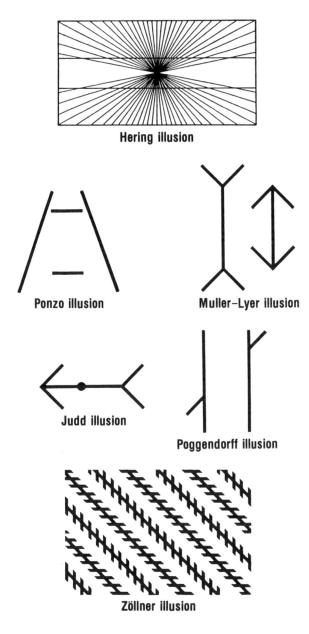

Figure 15: Famous illusions.

In the Müller-Lyer illusion the line with arrow-heads pointing away from the line appears to be shorter than the line where the arrowheads point toward the line. Is it really shorter? What happens if you redraw this illusion and change the angle at which the arrowheads meet the line? At some angle does the illusion fade or disappear? Are there things you see in the natural world that give rise to the Müller-Lyer illusion?

In the Poggendorf illusion the "pin" through the "straw" is actually a straight line. If you don't believe it, place a ruler along the diagonal line. You'll see the parts belong to the same straight line. Can you make a three-dimensional Poggendorf illusion using a wide soda straw and a pin? Using a clay cylinder and a long, thin stick? How does the distance between the vertical lines and the length of the diagonal line affect the illusion? What happens to the illusion when you invert it? When you turn it 90 degrees?

Another way to do the Poggendorf illusion is to draw an additional lower line that looks as if it is in line with the upper diagonal. People will invariably pick the wrong line as the one that lines up with the upper end.

The dot in the Judd illusion is at the midpoint of the line. Would a line give the same effect as a dot? Will the angle between the line and the arrowhead and tail affect the illusion?

Do the long lines in the Zöllner illusion appear to be parallel? Well, they are. If you don't believe it, measure their separation at different points. What happens to the illusion if you move the book farther away from your eyes? Do the lines appear to be more nearly parallel if you look at them from the ends of the lines with the book tilted back away from your eye? Can you find some angle of viewing that gives the illusion a three-dimensional effect?

Will you still see this illusion if you draw the parallel lines in an up-and-down direction rather than diagonally? Try it. Is the illusion more effective if the black lines appear on a colored background? How about colored lines on a black background? Does the angle at which the shorter lines cross the long parallel lines affect the illusion? If so, what angle gives the best illusion?

Zöllner thought that the illusion was the result of our being able to see diverging lines more easily than parallel lines. Can you disprove Zöllner on the basis of the drawings you made when you changed the angle of the crossing lines? Others have tried to explain Zöllner's illusion as being due to the curvature of the retina. The curvature makes some angles appear too large and others too small.

In Hering's illusion the two long horizontal lines are actually parallel. But the crossing lines cause the lines to appear bent. Could this be due to lateral inhibition? Some other illusions closely related to Hering's are shown in Figure 16. Notice how the direction of the crossing lines can change the direction of the "bowing." Notice also how the shape of the square and circle appear to be affected by the lines in the surrounding circles. What happens to the illusion if you view it with the book tilted back away from your eyes? Is the illusion as strong ·when you hold the book farther from your eyes?

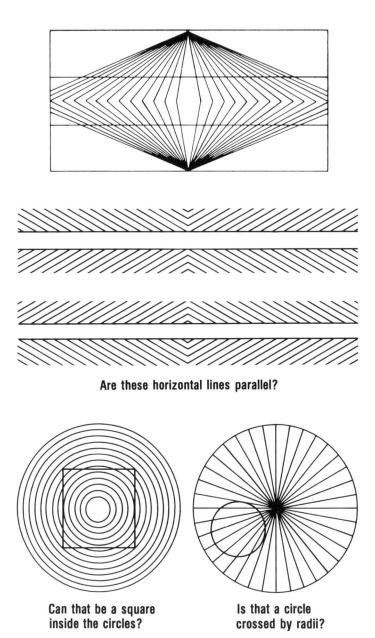

Are these horizontal lines parallel?

Can that be a square inside the circles?

Is that a circle crossed by radii?

Figure 16: Modified versions of Hering's illusion.

WHERE ARE THE ILLUSIONS? • Some people think that the line illusions you have seen are due to effects that take place in the eye. Others believe the illusions depend on the way our brains perceive the impulses coming from the retina. One way to find out is to draw these illusions using color. For example, make the vertical lines red and the horizontal lines green. Then make a pair of cardboard spectacles. Cover the opening in front of one eye with a red filter. Cover the other opening with a green filter. Be sure that you cannot see the red line through the red filter or the green line through the green filter. If you can, you will have to change either the filters or the color of the lines you use. Sometimes a cyan filter added to a green one will make the green line invisible.

In the case of the simple inverted T, the vertical red line will not be seen in the eye covered with a red filter. This is because a white background viewed through a red filter will appear red. Consequently, the red line cannot be distinguished from the red background. The horizontal green line appears black through the red filter because the red filter will not allow green light to pass through. Therefore the green line appears to be black on a red background. For similar reasons, the other eye will see the vertical line as black on a green background.

Examine each of the illusions through your colored spectacles. Remember, each eye receives only part of the illusion. Can you still see the illusion through the colored spectacles? If you can, the cause of the illusion must be in the brain. Why?

Here's another two-colored pattern that you can make. On white paper make a 2-inch (5 cm) by 2-inch grid of vertical green stripes and horizontal red stripes. Make the green stripes about an eighth of an inch (0.3 cm) wide and 2 inches long. Leave white stripes of the same width between them. If you use paint, wait until it dries. Then complete the grid by painting the horizontal red stripes in the same way. Now look at this grid through the red-and-green spectacles that you made. When you view this grid, what will be the color of the image on your right eye? On your left eye? Can your brain fuse these two images into a single pattern, or does it keep shifting?

ILLUSIONS OF AREAS • Draw some line figures that enclose equal areas. You might draw a square, a circle, a diamond, various rectangles, and triangles. Then ask people which figure encloses the greatest and the smallest area. Do any of them think the areas are equal? Which figures do they see as enclosing the greatest and the smallest area?

MOVING LINE ILLUSIONS • Copy and enlarge, or draw, the spiral shown in Figure 17. If possible, make it large enough to fit on a record-player turntable. What do you see when the spiral spins clockwise? For best viewing, put the turntable on the floor and watch the spiral spin from above. Does the rate at which it spins affect the illusion?

Now get ready for this one! After you turn off the turntable, continue to watch the spiral when it is still. What do you see?

Since you can't spin the spiral in two directions on a turntable, tape the spiral to a round sheet of cardboard.

Figure 17: Spin this spiral.

Then put it on a pin and spin it. If you spin it counter-clockwise, is anything different?

SUBJECTIVE CONTOURS • Look at Figure 18. You will see a white triangle that appears a brighter white than its white background. Its corners are located in the three black "pac men." The sides or contours of the bright-white triangle are called subjective contours because they aren't there. Yet, we see the triangle as if it had sides. It appears to be covering the triangle outlined with black lines. Gaetano Kanizsa brought illusions involving subjective contours to the attention of many in 1976. This illusion is known as the "Kanizsa triangle."

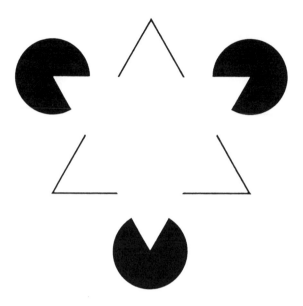

Figure 18: Subjective contours make this bright white Kanizsa triangle visible.

If you were to reverse the black and white in Figure 18, would you see a black triangle, darker than its dark background, covering parts of three white pac men and a triangle outlined in white? Try it! What do you find?

Make three dots on a sheet of paper. The dots should all be at equal distances from one another. How do you see the dots? As the corners of a triangle? Points on a circle? Or some other configuration? Most people see the dots as a triangle connected by three invisible straight lines.

Draw a wide, yellow circle on a sheet of paper. Then draw a black rectangle that extends upward from about the middle of the circle to about one radius beyond the circle. Draw it so that the top part of the circle seems to lie in front of the rectangle. Then draw a smaller yellow circle that seems to have its lower quarter hidden by the upper part of the rectangle. You now see a small yellow circle partly covered by a black rectangle. The larger circle seems to lie above the rectangle. Now paint both circles black to match the rectangle. What has changed? Which figure seems to be uppermost now? Do you see subjective contours? Where are they?

Copy Figure 18. Then see if you can make subjective "triangles" that have curved sides. The best way is to change the size and shape of the pac men's mouths. Also change the lengths of the black lines in the triangle that appear to lie under the subjective one. These lines should meet the subjective lines that connect with the pac men to form the subjective contours.

Once you get the hang of it, see if you can make other curved subjective shapes using your own designs. Subjective figures are not limited to the world of pac men. Can you use subjective contours to create the famous illusions shown in Figure 15?

Some people believe subjective contours result from contrast enhancement. The triangle appears brighter than its background because its corners are next to a black surface. Such enhancement is often present when a light surface lies next to a dark one. For example, remember the gray circle on the black-and-white background in the photograph in chapter 2?

However, look at Figure 19. Very little black is present and yet the illusion of contour is still there. The drawings in Figure 20 were devised by John M. Kennedy of the University of Toronto. In the first three, one might argue that the contrast is created by the ends of the

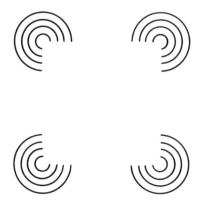

Figure 19: Even without the solid black ''pac men,'' this square with subjective contours is clearly visible.

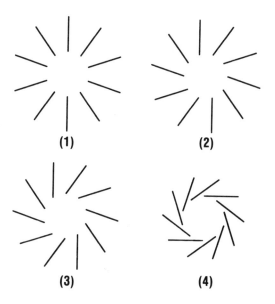

(1)

(2)

(3)

(4)

Figure 20: Subjective circles. Notice the bright circles in the center of drawings 1, 2, and 3. What happened to 4?

dark lines. However, if that's the case, why don't we see a bright area at the other ends of the lines? Perhaps we see the subjective circles in these illusions because the lines appear to run under the bright-white circle. In fact, in all the cases we've seen, the subjective figure seems to lie over something else. Further, the figures are always simple and regular ones with which we are familiar. In the fourth drawing of Figure 20 the illusion disappears. Can you explain why?

W. Ehrenstein first investigated the illusions shown in Figure 21. As you can see from Figure 21a, four lines are enough to create the subjective circle. Whether black or white, these circles seem to cover the intersecting lines. In Figure 21b Ehrenstein's lines create an interlocking grid of "streets" and circular intersections. Again, the streets seem to lie over the background.

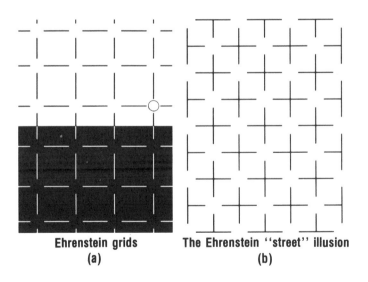

Ehrenstein grids
(a)

The Ehrenstein "street" illusion
(b)

Figure 21: Circles from straight lines.

What happens if you cover the illusions in Figure 21 with a transparent sheet of plastic that has randomly but closely packed dots on it? What happens when you drag the transparent sheet of dots across the illusion? Does the direction in which you drag the transparency make a difference?

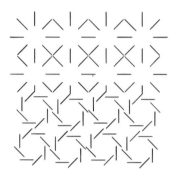

Figure 22: Where are the circles? This pattern was devised by Alex Stewart Fraser of the University of Cincinnati.

But look at Figure 22, which was developed by Alex Stewart Fraser of the University of Cincinnati in 1983. There you see the subjective circles and noncircles of Figure 20. However, what happens as you move the drawing away from your eye? Or what happens if you squint while looking at the picture? There is obviously a lot we don't know about subjective contours and most other illusions as well.

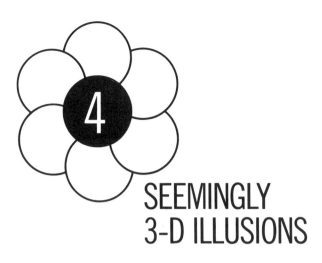

SEEMINGLY 3-D ILLUSIONS

We live in a three-dimensional world, but the retinas of our eyes have only two dimensions. Consequently, we perceive depth by inference. Through experience we learn a variety of cues that help us to infer the distance to the objects that we see. We learn to make the best bet about the world based on these cues.

Near objects cast larger images on the retina than distant objects. Objects that hide parts of other objects are closer than the objects they hide. Distant objects are generally higher in our visual field; that is, we look up to see them. Brighter objects are usually closer. Near objects cast sharper shadows than distant ones. The extent of contraction of the eye muscles used in focusing images provides clues about the distance to the object seen. So do the muscles that turn the eyes inward to see objects that are close by.

Distant objects show less parallax than near objects. Parallax is the apparent shift of an object when viewed from different positions. For example, hold your thumb upward at arm's length in front of your eyes. Now close first one eye and then the other. Notice how your thumb seems to shift relative to more distant objects. Now place a second thumb about halfway out to the other one. When you again close first one eye and then the other, the near thumb seems to shift more than the far one.

Unlike animals that have their eyes on the sides of their heads, we can see an object with both eyes. However, because our eyes are separated by an inch or two, (2.5–5 cm) the view we see with one eye is a little different from the one we see with the other. Normally, each eye sees very nearly the same image. But what happens if you push gently on the side of one eye? How many images do you see now? Impulses generated on the right side of both eyes travel to the right side of the brain. Similarly, nerve impulses that originate on the left side of both eyes travel to the left side of the brain. In the brain the images are somehow fused to form a single image. Because we see a little farther around one side of an object with one eye and a little farther around the other side of the object with the opposite eye, we get a sense of depth from the regions of the image that don't overlap.

To see how helpful this depth perception is, try reaching for objects with one eye closed. You might also like to see how well you can detect the location of sounds with just one ear. Put some cotton in one ear and spend some time in a safe place trying to locate the sounds you hear.

Light that has passed through haze becomes bluish. The farther away something is, the more haze lies between it and the viewer. That's why distant mountains appear blue. Consequently, artists use blue to give the illusion of depth in their paintings. People new to the western Rockies have difficulty estimating distance because there is so little haze. A distant snow-covered peak in the Rockies appears much closer than it really is to someone who grew up in the Smoky Mountains or the Adirondacks.

PERSPECTIVE AND ILLUSIONS • Another cue to perceiving depth is perspective. Parallel lines, such as railroad tracks, seem to converge in the distance. The far end of a long rectangular field appears to be narrower than the closer end. The distant poles in a long fence appear shorter than the near ones. Artists make good use of perspective in bringing a sense of depth to their paintings or drawings. So do those who draw illusions, as you can see from Figure 23. Design some illusions of your own that make use of perspective.

Figure 24 is a three-dimensional drawing with impossible perspective. The object drawn cannot be perceived. Find a book of engravings by the Dutch artist M.C. Escher. He has painted a variety of scenes that defy perspective.

Figure 25 appears to be a spiral that draws your eye to the center and gives us an illusion of depth. But if you study the drawing carefully, you'll see that it is really a series of smaller and smaller circles.

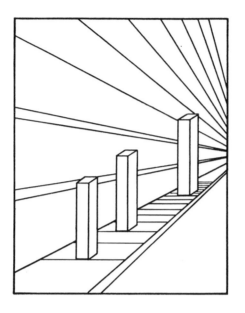

Figure 23: Can you believe these vertical objects
are all the same height?

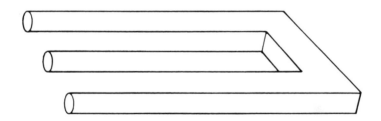

Figure 24: An impossible object.

Figure 25: It only looks like a spiral.

Could the Ponzo illusion (Figure 15) be the result of perspective? How about the Müller-Lyer illusion in Figure 15?

Some investigators have made the Müller-Lyer illusion from luminous wire and suspended it in a dark room. When viewed in this manner, it does appear to be three-dimensional.

Some people believe our eyes move outward along the line when we look at the figure on the left in the Müller-Lyer illusion and that this "stretches" the line. On the other hand, when we view the other figure, our eyes tend to look to the middle of the line, causing it to "shrink." Suppose you turn the Müller-Lyer illusion 90 degrees and look at it. Does the illusion still exist? Perhaps the line that was formerly on the left is now seen as a distant horizon. But what about the other line?

BINOCULAR-VISION ILLUSIONS • Hold your hand in a "thumbs up" position at arm's length in front of your eye. If you turn your eyes inward to look at your nearby thumb, you will see a single image of that thumb. But if you gaze across the thumb to focus your eyes on a more distant object, you will see two images of your thumb. With your eyes looking straight ahead, the images of the thumb falling on right and left retinas do not fall on corresponding regions. Consequently, you see two images of your one thumb. (Close one eye and one of those images will disappear.) For the same reason, if you turn your eyes inward again to look at your thumb, you will see double images of distant objects.

To see a "hot dog" illusion, put the ends of your two index fingers together about a foot (30 cm) in front of your eyes. Now focus your eyes on a distant object. A fingerlike hot dog will appear between the ends of your index fingers. If you pull your fingers just a little bit apart, the hot dog will "float" before your eyes. The hot dog is part of the region where the images overlap. You can see that this is true by closing first one eye and then the other. You'll see the image seen by each eye. Where do the images overlap?

Hold a paper tube to one eye and focus both eyes on a distant object. If you're holding the tube in front of your right eye, move your left hand, at arm's length, slowly toward the paper tube. You'll find a point where you seem to have a hole in your hand. Again, by closing first one eye and then the other, you'll see that there are two images. The image of your hand falls on the center of your left retina. The image of the distant object falls on the center of your right retina. The paper tube prevents light from the hand from reaching the right eye. As a result you see the hand as if it had a hole in it.

PERSISTENCE OF VISION ILLUSIONS • Your work with after-images has probably convinced you that images produced in the retina are retained there for some time. Of course, most images that you see are either not as bright as those used to produce after-images or are not viewed for as long. But the fact that you see the action in a motion picture or on a television screen as continuous motion indicates that ordinary pictures are retained on the retina for some time. This is known as persistence of vision. Brighter images persist longer than dimmer ones. And motion pictures shown at 48 frames per second are easily seen as continuous motion even though we are seeing a series of still pictures. In fact, the screen is dark half the time. The pictures on a television screen are "repainted" every sixtieth of a second. Yet, we see a 90-mph (145-kph) fastball as continuous motion on the TV screen. In ordinary light, we probably retain images on the retina for about a twentieth of a second.

To see an example of the persistence of vision, hold two pennies vertically between the tips of your two index fingers. Then rub the pennies against one another in short, rapid, up-and-down motion. You will see a third coin between the other two. Does the third coin appear to be above the other two, or below them? Does it ever appear on the other side?

Draw a picture of a bird cage on one side of a card. Draw a bright-yellow-and-red canary on the other side. Cut a little notch at the top of a wooden dowel and fasten the card to the dowel. When you rotate the card swiftly by spinning the dowel rapidly back and forth between your hands, the canary will appear to be in the cage. You could also put a fish in a bowl or a cat in a tree.

You can make a simple movie of your own too. Take two pieces of paper, each about 3 inches by 6 inches (7.5 by 15 cm). Tape them together at one narrow end to make a two-sheet pad. Draw a smiling face on the lower sheet. Now let the upper sheet fall onto the lower one. You should be able to see at least the outline of the face you have drawn through the upper sheet. Copy the outline of the smiling face on the upper sheet but draw a frown on this face. Roll the upper sheet with the frowning face (curling it upward) around a pencil to make a paper tube. Hold the taped end of the two-sheet pad with one hand. Use your other hand to rapidly move the pencil from one end of the pad to the other along the upper, curled sheet. This will cause the upper sheet to curl and uncurl again and again. The result will be a simple motion picture.

If you enjoy this simple movie, you might like to make a longer "film." Use a pad of paper to make a series of stick-figure drawings (or more detailed drawings if you have the patience) that show a figure running, throwing a ball, making a layup shot, or some other action. By flipping the pages of the pad, you'll be able to see the action unfold.

If you have a slide projector, project a scene from a slide on a dark sheet of paper. You won't be able to see the picture. But if you have someone wave a white stick rapidly across the screen, the scene will become visible.

STOPPING MOTION • If you've ever seen a strobe light operating in an otherwise dark room, you know that the light can produce some strange effects. We see people only when the light is on. As a result, we see them in one position and then in another. We can't see the motion that brought them from one position to the next.

You can make a stroboscope of your own and use it to stop motion. Take a round sheet of cardboard about a foot (30 cm) in diameter. **Ask an adult to use a knife to cut out the cardboard and eight equally spaced slits along the circumference of the cardboard circle.** Each slit should be about half an inch (1.25 cm) wide and an inch and a half (3.75 cm) long. Finally, have the adult cut a hole that will fit your index finger about 3 inches (7.5 cm) out from the center of the disk. You can use a tack to fasten the stroboscope to one end of a wooden dowel as shown in Figure 26.

Watch a spinning fan (**but don't get too close**) or bicycle wheel as you turn your stroboscope. You'll find that you can make these turning objects appear to stand still. If you turn your strobe around 2 times per second, you will view the object 16 times per second. If the object is spinning at the same rate, then you'll see the object in the same position each time you view it. Will the spinning object still appear stopped if it is turning at 32 or 64 times per second? What will you see if it's turning 8 times per second? If you have managed to

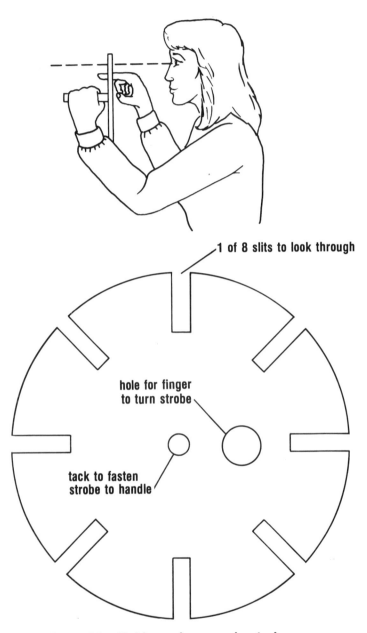

1 of 8 slits to look through

hole for finger
to turn strobe

tack to fasten
strobe to handle

Figure 26: Making a homemade stroboscope.

"stop" a spinning object with your strobe, how can you tell whether you're seeing it after every turn, every second turn, or every third or more turns?

To make things that are turning at rather slow rates appear stopped, you may have to cover every other slit so that you only get four glimpses per turn of the strobe. Can you see now why the wagon wheels in western movies sometimes appear to be stopped? Can you explain why they may appear to turn slowly backward or forward?

3-D REVERSAL ILLUSIONS • Like the Necker cube, there are a variety of illusions that are referred to as reversals. If you stare at them for a while, you will see that they can be perceived in more than one logical way. Since the brain can't decide which is the "best bet" because all are reasonable, we keep perceiving them in different ways. Our perception reverses back and forth. Several such three-dimensional reversals are shown in Figure 27.

One of the drawings in Figure 27, the one that can be seen as a folded card or an opening book, can easily be done with a real card. Fold the card in half. Let it spring back to its natural partially opened condition. Hold the card at arm's length with the crease farthest from your eyes. Or place the card on a chair, open side toward you. Stare through the card and you will perceive it in two ways. It can be a "tent" or an inside corner.

MOTION AND ILLUSIONS • Have you ever been sitting in a car at a red light when the car beside you started to move slowly forward? You may have thought the car you

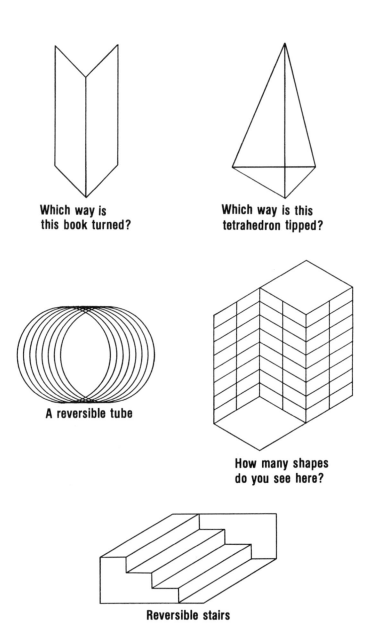

Which way is
this book turned?

Which way is this
tetrahedron tipped?

A reversible tube

How many shapes
do you see here?

Reversible stairs

Figure 27: Reversible figures.

were in was moving backward. It's a very common illusion of motion. Similarly, sitting in a train it's difficult to know whether it's your train that's moving or the one on the next set of tracks.

Recent studies, however, have shown that we tend to perceive the world in a logical way as far as motion is concerned. For example, a subject is shown two dots on a screen. In the next frame, which occurs in a fraction of a second, the two dots are shown displaced to the right. The subject always perceives the two dots as moving along parallel paths from left to right. However, the dots could just as well have moved in a crossing pattern. But we know from experience that if the two objects were to cross, they would collide and their paths would change. Further, we know that if two bodies are in motion they will continue moving in the same direction unless a force is applied to change that motion.

Watch a waterfall for a minute or two. Then look at the bank of the stream at the foot of the fall. The water will appear to be running backward. Is this a logical way to view motion? Certainly such motion is an illusion. Do you think it's related to the effects you saw after watching the rotating spiral in Chapter 3?

You may not be able to watch a waterfall, but you can watch a record turntable. Stare at the center of a turntable for a full minute. Then have someone turn it off while you continue to stare at the center point. You will see the turntable turn slowly in the other direction.

Watch a rolling bicycle wheel. What path does the rim of the wheel seem to follow? If you think it's a circle, you're mistaken. To find the actual path, fix a marking pen or a piece of chalk to a wheel or a round sheet of cardboard. Then roll the wheel or disk along next to a blackboard or a long sheet of cardboard. The pen or chalk will mark the path of the wheel's rim. How would you describe the path made by the rolling wheel?

From a safe distance, watch a wheel as it rolls along the highway. You may be able to see the wheel appear to stand still as if you were using a stroboscope. If you wear eyeglasses, you are more likely to see the effect if you tap your glasses. If you don't, the effect may arise if you jerk your head or walk along the ground. The natural jerky movements of your eyes may cause them to move at the same rate as the car's wheel for a short time. During that time the wheel will appear to be at rest because your eye is moving in parallel with it.

Ask a friend to ride his or her bike along a path or sidewalk that you can easily observe. As the bike approaches, fix your sight on a point you have asked your friend to ride over. You will find that as the bottom of the wheel rolls over the point your eyes are fixed on, you can see the moving spokes quite clearly. To understand why you can see the spokes so clearly, think of the path followed by the rim of a wheel. At what point is the rim moving slowest?

The Pulfrich pendulum is another illusion of motion. To see this illusion you will need a piece of string, a thumbtack, a paper clip, and some white clay or some clay and white tape. Make and suspend the pendulum as shown in Figure 28. Watch the bob swing back and forth at the end of a string about a foot (30 cm) long. Cover *one* eye with one side of a pair of sunglasses or a colored plastic filter. Now watch the pendulum with both eyes. You will see the pendulum bob appear to move along an

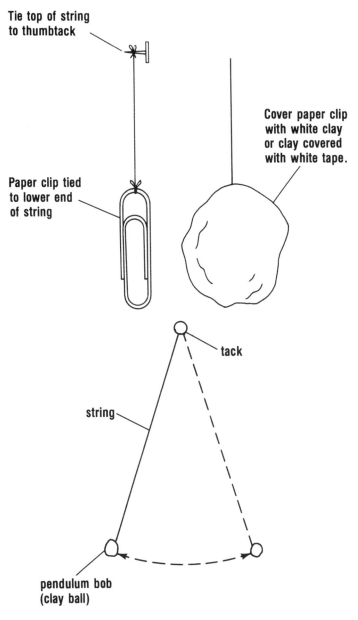

Tie top of string
to thumbtack

Cover paper clip
with white clay
or clay covered
with white tape.

Paper clip tied
to lower end
of string

tack

string

pendulum bob
(clay ball)

Figure 28: A Pulfrich pendulum.

elliptical path rather than along the nearly linear path that the pendulum actually follows.

Because the cover over one eye reduces the intensity of the light in that eye, it is believed that the nerve cells fire later than the cells in the other eye. Therefore, the signals sent to the brain from the covered eye are delayed relative to those from the other eye. The net effect is that we perceive the motion as curved rather than along a line.

Finally, you can induce a stationary object to appear to move. To see this effect, watch a glowing cigarette on an ashtray from across an otherwise totally dark room. **If you can't find an adult who will provide a cigarette and supervise the experiment,** you can use the small red light on an electronic device such as a telephone answering machine. The light itself is probably too bright, but if you cover it with a card that has a pinhole in it, the intensity should be about right.

Stand at the other side of the (dark) room from the small light and stare at it. After a while you will probably begin to see it move in an erratic fashion. If you don't, try increasing the tension in all the muscles on one side of your body. Or turn your eyes to one side as far as you can and keep them there for a few seconds. Then look back at the light. Does it begin to move?

Some people think this effect has to do with the fatigue of the eye muscles. Normally our eyes are in constant jerky motion to avoid the empty-field effect discussed in Chapter 2. To keep the eyes fastened on the small light requires that the muscles remain fixed at the same degree of contraction for a long time. The fatigue of these eye muscles somehow changes the actual signals sent to the brain, causing us to see a motion that isn't there. Perhaps any muscle tension can induce this effect. If that is the case, then we can understand why tensing the muscles of the body induces the illusion.

ILLUSIONS IN THE NATURAL WORLD

We tend to think of illusions as lines on paper that produce odd effects and fool our senses. However, as you will see, there are plenty of illusions in the natural world, too. Just close your eyes. Even without after-images, you still see spots of light. In a deep forest where there is no sound, you will still hear the "ring of silence." Your brain is so eager for impulses from the sense organs that it seems to invent some if none are there.

When you watch a sunset, you see a sun that is red. Yet that same sun was not red a few minutes earlier. What happened? Has the sun really changed its color in such a short time? Of course it hasn't. But as another day draws to a close, the sun's light has to pass through more and more atmosphere. This is

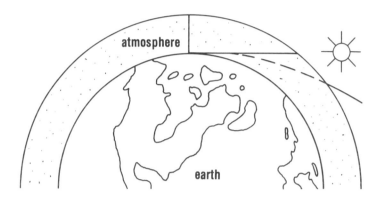

Figure 29: The path of sunlight through the earth's atmosphere.

shown in Figure 29. The solid lines reveal the relative distance that light travels through the atmosphere at midday and near sunset. The dotted line shows the path of sunlight refracted by the earth's atmosphere at sunset. It reveals why the sun is visible even after it is below the horizon.

Some of the sunlight passing through the earth's atmosphere is absorbed by molecules of air, water, dust, and other small particles. These particles then reradiate the light. (This process is called scattering.) However, the light that the particles radiate travels in all directions. Its motion is not limited to the straight-line path from sun to earth that it was following before it was absorbed. Because blue light is scattered about ten times as much as red light, the light that comes through the long atmospheric path to our eyes at sunset is mostly red. Much of the light in the blue end of the spectrum has been scattered off the path that would have brought it to our eyes. As a result, most of the light that reaches our eyes at sunset consists of the longer unscattered wavelengths of light—the light that we perceive as red, orange, and yellow.

At midday, when sunlight travels through a shorter length of atmosphere, less light is scattered. The sun appears yellow instead of red because smaller amounts of light from the blue end of the spectrum are scattered than at sunset. In space, where there are very few particles to scatter light, the sun is seen to be white.

It is the blue light scattered by the atmosphere during the daytime that makes the sky appear blue. Some of the light scattered by the atmosphere is absorbed by other particles and reradiated again. Thus the light that comes to us from the sky is blue. Consequently, to us the sky appears to be blue. But, in fact, it has no color. The true color of the atmosphere can be seen at night. It's black! Astronauts in space see a black sky.

MAKING A SUNSET AND A BLUE "SKY" OF YOUR OWN • To duplicate a sunset and its surrounding blue sky, fill a large fish tank with water. Shine a beam of light from a slide projector through the water. On the side opposite the light source you can see the "sun" shining through the "atmosphere." Now, to scatter the light you can add a small amount of powdered milk or dairy substitute to the water. Stir the white powder into the water. Then look at your sun. Has it changed at all? Continue to add and stir the powder, a small amount at a time, until the sun becomes red. If you look at the water (atmosphere) around the sun, you will see that it is blue because of scattering.

WHEN DOES THE SUN REALLY SET? • In Figure 29 the dotted line shows the actual path of sunlight through the atmosphere at sunset. The path is not straight but curved. When light passes from one transparent medium to another, it is bent (refracted). You can see this for yourself by sticking a spoon into a glass of water. At the point where the spoon enters the water it appears to be broken. Light coming from the part of the spoon that is submerged is bent when it leaves the water. Light from the part of the spoon above the water comes straight to our eye. Therefore, the two parts of the spoon appear to be separated. Can you now explain why a brook or a swimming pool always looks more shallow than it really is?

The light coming through space from the sun is bent by the earth's atmosphere. The bending is gradual because the atmosphere becomes denser closer to the earth's surface. As you can see in Figure 29, the sun is actually below the horizon when we see it setting. To see a similar effect, put a coin on the bottom of a teacup. Look over the rim of the cup to see the coin. Then lower your eyes until the coin just disappears from your sight. Ask someone to slowly and carefully, so as not to disturb the coin, pour water into the cup. The coin will reappear. Light coming from the coin through the water is bent toward your eye, making the coin visible. Without the water to bend it, this light could not reach your eye.

A photograph of the setting sun reveals that the shape of the sun itself appears to change at sunset. This too is because of refraction. The sun itself has a diameter of 0.50 degree. This means it occupies $1/360$th of the 180-degree angle between the eastern and western horizons. At sunset, light from the bottom of the sun passes through a greater length of atmosphere than does light from the top. As a result, it is bent more than the light from the upper part of the sun. In fact, the lower edge of the setting sun appears to be 0.58 degree higher than it actually is. The upper edge, however, is only 0.48 degree higher. As a result, the sun is "flattened" by about 0.10 degree. Therefore, the sun's vertical diameter at sunset is about 20 percent less than its horizontal diameter.

MIRAGES • Have you ever seen a mirage? They are more common than you think. And you don't have to be on a desert to see one. On a hot summer day you can find plenty of mirages on the highway. As you drive up a long, straight incline, you may well see what looks like a lake at the top of the rise. What you are seeing is light from the sky that is refracted by the hot air above the pavement. Light passing through this hot air may produce visible inverted images of objects that lie beyond the horizon. On the hot plains an inverted image of a city's skyline may be seen on a farm far from the city.

Because of the curvature of the earth, the ocean or flatland drops away from a horizontal line at a rate of 16 feet (4.8 m) every 5 miles (8 km). Consequently, nor-

The sun shortly after sunrise. Compare its horizontal diameter to its vertical diameter. Does the shape of the sun also flatten at sunset?

A mirage: "Silver Dry Lake" in
the Mojave Desert, California.

mally even tall ships are not visible from more than a few miles away. However, when the air next to the ground or ocean is colder than the air above, light is bent downward. As a result, we can often see objects that would normally be below the horizon. The image of a ship may appear above the ship itself. Such an effect is called *looming*. People on the ship, in turn, may be able to see a lighthouse from a distance of 40 miles (64 km).

Here's a mirage you can observe on a hot day if you can find a long (30 feet—9 m—or more) flat wall that faces south. You should stand at one end of the wall with your face against its surface. Have someone at the other end hold a spoon or a key near the wall. When the object is moved slowly toward the wall, you may be able to see an image of the object that appears to lie behind the wall.

Another place to see images is across smooth, hard sand at a beach when there is little wind. Place your chin on the sand so that your eyes are as close to the ground as possible. Raise and lower your head very slowly as you look along the surface of the flat sand. You may be able to see a "lake" on the sand that brings to your eyes light from objects that are 100 feet (30 m) or so away.

TWINKLE, TWINKLE LITTLE STAR • Stars are said to twinkle. Twinkling is the result of starlight passing through various layers of air with different temperatures. At times, light from the star is brought together making the star appear brighter. At other times, the layers of air tend to diverge the light, making the star appear less bright. Similarly, the color of the star may vary. A prism spreads white light into a spectrum because different colors (wavelengths) are refracted differently. The light from a star has a variety of colors. Sometimes the light is refracted so that we see its red light; at other times the light refracted by the atmosphere places the star's blue light on our eyes.

As you might guess, stars twinkle more near the horizon because the starlight has to pass through more layers of atmosphere. You may also notice that planets do not twinkle as much as stars. Can you explain why?

LOOKING AT LIGHT IN YOUR ENVIRONMENT • Find a showcase electric light bulb (a clear bulb with a long, straight vertical filament). If you look at light coming from the bulb through a very narrow slit, you will see a series of bright and dark bands. The bright bands, particularly the ones farthest from the center, may contain some colors. If you look at the light with your eyes nearly closed, the light will have to pass through the narrow spaces between your eyelashes. Again you will see bands of light and darkness. The light bands reveal the colors of the spectrum. You are seeing the effects of diffraction and interference. When light passes through a narrow opening it spreads out. In some places the waves cancel each other, causing dark lines. In other areas the light waves reinforce each other, giving rise to bright bands. Because the waves from light of different wavelengths reinforce at slightly different places, we see the colors of the spectrum in the interference pattern. What appears to be an illusion is simply the way natural light behaves.

○ Look at a distant streetlamp. You may see a streak of light extending from the top or bottom of the light. The streak arises from light that is refracted by the tears that line your eyelids. If you lower your upper lid until it is at the top of your pupil, the effect will be very noticeable.

○ If you've ever seen the moon or sun rise or set over a large lake or the ocean, you may have noticed a long band of light that extends along the water toward the horizon. Why do we see a band of diffuse light rather than an image of the sun or moon?

The surface of the water is not smooth. Only the side of each wave that faces us can reflect light to our eyes. The light striking the wave at the correct angle does just that. Instead of seeing light reflected from a single mirror, we see light reflected from thousands of water mirrors. But the waves are continually changing and so the light we see is continually shifting from wave to wave.

○ For a somewhat similar reason, a freshly mowed lawn has alternate bright and dark bands. Can you explain why?

○ On a bright, sunny day look at the small circles of light found in the shade of a tree that has lots of leaves. How can there be circles of light in the shade? What you see are pinhole images of the sun made by small openings between the leaves. To see a single pinhole image of the sun, make a small hole in a card. Hold a second card beneath the one with the pinhole. Light coming through the hole in the card will fall on this second card. You will find an image of the sun on the screen below the pinhole.

How does this photograph illustrate the fact that the water in this pond is not perfectly flat? Turn the picture upside down. The barn and trees will appear as they might if you looked at them across a parking lot on a hot summer day. Why do you see such an illusion?

A freshly mowed lawn has alternate bright and
dark bands, depending on the angle at which sunlight is reflected by the grass blades.

What happens to the size of the images as you move the second card closer and then farther from the pinhole?

○ Now turn the pinhole effect around. Take a small square mirror and use it to reflect sunlight. Hold a screen close to the mirror to "capture" the reflected light. You will see a square patch of light. But what happens if you reflect the light onto a distant screen such as the side of a building a hundred or more feet (30 m) away? Why does the reflected beam become circular?

○ Look at some print through a tube made from a rolled-up sheet of paper. Does the print seem clearer? Will the tube enable you to see things across a room more clearly? Will it allow you to see objects on a faraway hill more clearly?

○ Falling snowflakes seen from below appear dark, not white. This is because the lower sides of the flakes do not reflect as much light as they do when we view them on the ground. They therefore appear much darker than the brighter, though cloudy, sky.

Once on the ground, the snow may appear brighter than a uniformly gray sky. But how can this be true? It isn't! If you place a mirror that reflects the sky next to the snow, it will be obvious that the sky is far brighter. But why did the snow look so bright in the first place? Again, compared with surrounding woods, shrubs, and buildings, the snow is much brighter. It is the contrast between snow and darker objects that makes it appear so much brighter than it really is.

○ If you view the roofs of a row of houses against the brighter background of a sky at dusk, you may see a bright border along the edge of the roofs. Could this effect be related to the Mach bands that you saw in Chapter 2?

THE MOON ILLUSION • Probably the best-known and most widely seen natural illusion is the rising moon. On the horizon, the moon appears to be considerably larger than it does when viewed at its zenith (its highest point in the sky). People have been aware of this illusion since the beginning of history. Ptolemy, an early astronomer from Alexandria, Egypt, believed that the moon appeared larger on the horizon because we compare it with distant trees and buildings. The size of the moon's image on our retinas may be as large as those made by trees and buildings on the horizon. Since we know the moon is farther away than those objects, we perceive it as very large. It's similar to an after-image. If we adjust our eyes to view an after-image on a distant wall, it appears much larger than it does on a nearby surface. However, the moon illusion exists when the moon rises on the ocean, where there are no houses or trees to form images of comparative size. Consequently, many people have looked for other explanations.

You can prove to yourself that the moon's size really doesn't change, despite what your senses tell you. Simply photograph the moon on the horizon and at various points along its path until it reaches its zenith. What do you find when you measure these images on film? Or you could leave the camera shutter open and let the moon's image sweep out a light path across the film. Does the path swept out get narrower as the moon ascends?

Some people have suggested that the illusion has to do with how we view the moon. Things that are higher in our visual field are usually farther away. Therefore, we may see the risen moon as smaller because we subconsciously think it's farther away than a rising moon. You might test this idea in a number of ways. First, look at a rising moon normally. Then look at it with your chin on your chest. In this way you will be using the upper part of your visual field to see the moon. Is the illusion diminished when you do this?

In the same way, after the moon has risen 30 degrees or more, look at it with your head tilted back. In this way you will view the moon as if it were straight ahead or even in your lower visual field. You could also lie on your back and look at the moon high in the sky. Does the moon, when it is high in the sky, appear larger than normal if viewed as if it were straight ahead or in our lower visual field?

Nearly thirty years ago, Lloyd Kaufman and Irvin Rock asked people to subjectively compare the size of the moon's image at different altitudes. Their findings showed that generally people see a moon on the horizon as nearly 1.5 times larger than a moon at its zenith. Their results indicated that the elevation of the eyes had little or nothing to do with the apparent size of the moon.

Kaufman and Rock had subjects hold a sheet of cardboard with a hole up to the sky so they could see only the moon. When the moon was viewed through the cardboard, no houses or trees were seen. There was nothing with which the subject could compare the moon. What do you think they found? You can see for yourself by making a small hole in a sheet of cardboard that enables you to see only the rising moon. Look at the moon alone through the cardboard. Then look at the moon with its surrounding terrain. Does the size of the rising moon seem to change?

They also tested to see if the distance to the horizon had an effect. One horizon was 2 miles (3.2 km) away, the other was less than half a mile (0.8 km). Their results showed the illusion to be greater if the moon was seen over the more distant horizon.

They found that color and brightness seemed to have no effect on the illusion. However, an inverted horizon, one viewed from the position of a football center looking at a punter, seemed to reduce the illusion. Do you find this to be true?

When people look at the sky, most of them see it as a flattened dome. It does not appear to be a perfect hemisphere. Consequently, they see the horizon as more distant than the zenith. Is that the way you see the sky? Figure 30a shows the sky as most people see it and as the hemisphere that it actually is. (After all, the moon's distance from the center of the earth is almost constant during a twelve-hour period.)

To check up on this, ask a number of people to point to the place that they think marks the midpoint between the horizon and a point directly overhead. You can make a rough measurement of their estimate by finding how many fists you have to place on top of one another to get to the place they consider the midpoint. Each of your fists is probably about 10 degrees, as you can see in Figure 30b.

You'll probably find that most people underestimate the midpoint (45 degrees) considerably. They are

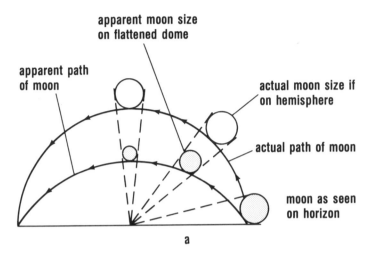

apparent moon size
on flattened dome

apparent path
of moon

actual moon size if
on hemisphere

actual path of moon

moon as seen
on horizon

a

b

First, line up top of your extended fist with the horizon. Then go fist on fist upward until you reach altitude indicated by subject. If 9 fists required to reach the zenith, each fist is worth 10 degrees.

Figure 30: The sky as it is and as we see it.

more likely to see it nearer 30 degrees than 45. This means that they really do see the sky as a flattened dome.

Are their estimates of the midpoint affected by clouds? That is, do they make a different estimate on a cloudy day than on a clear day? How about a partly cloudy day? What does this tell you about the apparent flattening of a cloud-covered sky and a clear one?

In Figure 30a you see the moon on the horizon, at the zenith, and somewhere in between those two points. Since we see the horizon as farther away than the zenith, we see the moon as larger on the horizon than anywhere else. The size of the moon's image on the retina is the same regardless of its altitude. But we assume the sky to be a flattened dome in which the horizon is farther from us than the zenith. Therefore, we perceive the moon to have its maximum size on the horizon because that's where we think it is farthest from us. Can you find evidence from your own experiments to support this idea, or does your data lead you toward another theory?

WEIGHT ILLUSIONS • Place some sand in a small jar. Place enough sand in a large box so that the box of sand and the jar of sand have the same weight. Use a balance scale to be sure they are equal. Now ask several subjects to hold the jar on one hand and the box on the other. Then ask them to tell you which is heavier. Almost everyone will think the jar is heavier. Do you find any exceptions? Can you explain this illusion?

Carry a heavy load, such as pails of water or heavy suitcases in one or both hands for a long time. When you put the load down, your hand(s) may automatically rise. Is this an example of lateral enhancement instead of the lateral inhibition discussed in Chapter 2? You may be able to get the same effect in another way. Stand in a doorway with your arms at your sides. Push against the door frame with the outside of your wrists for a few seconds. When you stop, you'll find that your arms tend to rise.

TEMPERATURE ILLUSIONS • Find three large plastic containers or pails. Put ice water in one, very warm water at about 110°F (45°C) in another, and room-temperature water (about 78°F, or 25°C) in the third. Place the fingers of one hand in the hot water. Put the fingers of your other hand in the cold water. Leave them there for a minute. Then place both hands in the water at room temperature and move your fingers around to sample the water temperature. How does the water feel to the hand that was in the cold water? To the hand that was in the hot water? Are fingers good thermometers? What do your hot and cold receptors tell you?

Place a lid from a metal can on a kitchen counter. Beside it, place a circular piece of cardboard that is the same size as the metal can lid. Leave both disks for about five minutes so they can come to room temperature. Now touch the cardboard with one hand and the metal with the other. Which one feels colder? Do you think it's really colder than the other one? To find out, attach one of them to a thermometer bulb with some tape. Allow it to sit for 5 minutes and record the temperature. Repeat the experiment with the other disk. Were their temperatures the same or were they different?

How can you explain the fact that the metal lid felt cool to your touch and the cardboard did not?

TOUCH AND TEMPERATURE ILLUSIONS • This touch illusion was first described by Aristotle more than two thousand years ago. Ask someone to cross her second finger over her index finger. With her eyes closed and fingers crossed, press a marble or a pencil against the top of her index finger, then against the top of her second finger, and finally in the gap between the ends of her two crossed fingers. Each time ask her how many pencils or marbles she feels. Then have someone do the same thing to you. When do you feel as though two things are touching you?

Find a hairpin. You'll see that you can hold the two ends of the pin at various separations. Ask a subject to close his eyes. Use the pins to touch (gently) various parts of your subject's arm and hand. How far apart do the ends of the pin have to be before he can detect two points of touch on the outside of his arm? On the inside of his arm? On his palm? On his fingers? What does this experiment tell you about the distance between touch receptors on your arm, hands, and fingers?

Use the point of a pencil to gently touch, at random, a variety of points along a subject's arm and the back of his hand. Usually he will feel a sensation of being touched. Does he ever feel a sensation of coldness? Warmth? Pain?

TASTE ILLUSIONS • One of the problems that astronauts have while living in space is that they can't taste their food very well. The fluids that normally drain out of our heads into the lower parts of our body don't do so in space. In a weightless environment there is no force to pull the liquids from the head. Astronauts feel as if they have head colds while in the weightlessness of space. Will they be able to taste things better if they stand on their heads?

○ Have you ever noticed how a drink that tasted very sweet when you took that first sip seems to lose its sweetness with time? Keep a concentrated solution of sugar water in your mouth for about 20 seconds. Then taste fresh water. Many people say the fresh water now tastes salty. Does it taste salty to you?

○ Make a cup of very sweet tea and sip it for a few minutes. Then eat a spoonful of jam. Now go back to sipping tea. Does the tea seem less sweet than it did before?

○ After eating an unsweetened grapefruit, try drinking some milk. Sour, isn't it? Now try the reverse. Drink some milk and then eat the grapefruit. Is there any difference?

○ Hot peppers may be difficult for you to eat. Try putting a little salt on your tongue first. Does it make them taste "cooler?"

○ Prepare some slices of an apple and a pear. Blindfold your subject and ask him to hold his nose. Place a piece of apple or pear on his tongue. Let him chew the fruit. Can he distinguish apple from pear? Between trials have him rinse his mouth with plain water.

Now repeat the experiment. This time he should be blindfolded, but he should not hold his nose. Can he distinguish apple from pear with his nose? With his tongue and mouth? If you hold a slice of pear beneath his nose while he eats an apple, which does he think he's eating?

You might like to repeat both these experiments using small pieces of apple and onion instead of pear. Are your results similar?

6

SCIENCE, ILLUSIONS, AND MAGICIANS

You've probably watched in amazement as a magician pulled rabbits from a hat, talked to a bodiless head, or sawed someone in half. Yet, you know perfectly well these are illusions. Rabbits don't grow in hats. A head cannot survive without its body. And no one could be sawed in half and then be put back together in a matter of seconds. Any good magician will tell you that he or she uses illusions or sleight-of-hand in performing the seemingly impossible feats that appear onstage.

When you watch a magician at work, see if you can figure out how each trick is done. Sit close to the stage but not in the center. Try to find a seat near the side of the stage. Look for reflections that seem abnormal, objects located in the wings of the stage, breaks in the stage floor that may reveal trapdoors. And try to concentrate on the space around the magician; don't watch his or her face.

RABBITS AND RIBBONS • Before pulling a rabbit from a hat, many magicians will pull seemingly endless lengths of ribbon from the same hat. While reaching for his top hat and bringing it close to his chest, he uses his other hand, which is screened from the audience, to place a roll of tightly wound paper into the hat. The roll, which the magician had concealed under his coat, is of a size that allows friction to keep it in place even when the hat is inverted. He then proceeds to pull the brightly colored paper or ribbon from the hat. While appearing to reinsert the vast amount of paper back into the hat, the magician grabs a bound rabbit (or duck or pigeon) that lies on a board behind his stage table. The animal, concealed by the colored ribbon, is inserted into the hat along with the paper. At a later time, the magician can reach into the hat, quickly untie the animal, and pull it out. There are other approaches to this trick, but all involve some sleight-of-hand.

SAWING SOMEONE IN HALF • Perhaps the best-known stage illusion is one in which a person is sawed in half and then put back together. The person, who is introduced by the magician, lies down in a box. His head sticks out one end of the box and his feet stick out the other. The magician and an assistant then use a large saw to cut the box in half. The two halves, with head and feet still apparent, are separated. After some magician patter, the two halves are put back together and the person emerges from the box in one piece.

The box is made of two halves. One person is hidden in the "foot" half of the box. The person who is to be sawed in half climbs into the "head" half of the box. As she puts her head through the opening in her half of the box, the other person, wearing identical shoes, puts her feet through the opening at the other end. Both people must bend their bodies so they fit into just half the box. The position is not comfortable, but the act doesn't take very long. After the sawing, the two people, on a verbal signal from the magician, pull their respective feet and head back into the boxes. The person who entered the box then emerges, leaving the other to suffer for a few moments longer until the box is moved offstage.

IT'S ALL DONE WITH MIRRORS • After some discussion about the head of a broken statue that suddenly came to life, a magician walks to a box that rests on a table. The box is opened and a person's head appears. A conversation between the bodiless head and the magician reveals the story of an unfortunate prince or princess who was condemned to imprisonment in a stone bust.

The illusion is created by means of mirrors, as shown in Figure 31. The magician's assistant, kneeling beneath the table, extends his or her head through the table into the bottomless box. Two mirrors at right angles screen the assistant's body while reflecting the uniform color of the floor and surrounding walls to the eyes of the audience. The table, therefore, appears to be open

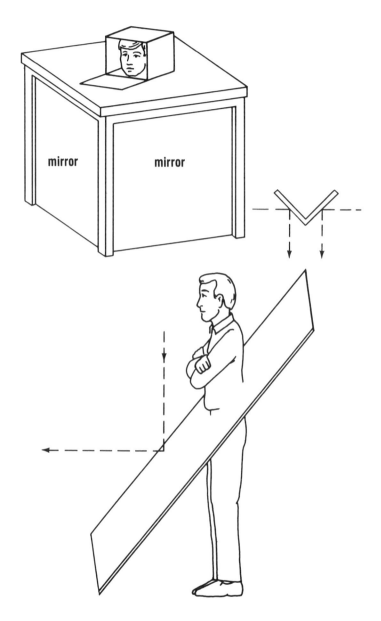

Figure 31: The bodiless head (top) and half-body (bottom) tricks.

beneath. Though only three legs of the table are visible, the audience assumes the rear leg is directly behind the near leg.

A similar technique, using a long mirror at an angle of 45 degrees, can be used to create the illusion of a half person floating above the floor.

Mirrors can be used also to create the illusion of ghosts on a stage. Such ghosts are referred to as Pepper's ghost in the theater because the effect was first devised by Professor John Henry Pepper of the London Polytechnic Institution in 1863. If you hold a lighted candle in front of a window at night, you will see the reflection of the candle and your hand. The image of the candle will appear to be as far behind the window as the actual candle is in front of it. By placing a large sheet of glass diagonally across a dark stage, the images of persons to the side of the stage who are clad in flowing white sheets and illuminated by a light will appear to the audience as ghosts.

Before you try to produce illusions on a stage, work first with a small model of your illusion. For example, before you create something like Pepper's ghost on a stage, try making a smaller ghost using a small pane of glass and a flashlight.

You might begin with this easy-to-make but fascinating illusion. Using a window pane **(be careful not to cut yourself)**, which you can buy in a hardware store, you can create a mirror illusion. The design for this illusion is shown in Figure 32. A lighted candle appears to be burning in a jar of water.

In addition to the apparent or virtual images that can be made with mirrors or sheets of glass, you can

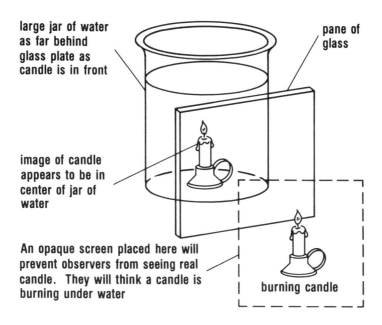

large jar of water as far behind glass plate as candle is in front

pane of glass

image of candle appears to be in center of jar of water

An opaque screen placed here will prevent observers from seeing real candle. They will think a candle is burning under water

burning candle

Figure 32: Light reflected from glass creates an image of a candle that appears to be burning in water.

create real images with concave mirrors and convex lenses. A real image is one that can be captured on a screen, one in which the rays of light that start from points on an object are brought together point for point in the image.

THE FLOATING LADY • The magician places a thick, flat board on the backs of two chairs. From the side of the stage enters a woman wearing a flowing gown and carrying a large, beautiful bouquet. She lies on the board as the magician walks behind it and passes his hands above the woman to show that there are no wires attached to the board or to the woman. He then speaks a series of mumbo-jumbo words that "hypnotize" his subject while his assistants remove the chairs from beneath the board. Lo and behold! the lady appears to float in midair. As the magician raises his hands, the lady and board ascend slowly only to descend as he lowers his hands. His assistants replace the chairs, and the magician, without touching lady or board, uses his hands to guide the board back to its original resting place.

The bouquet and gown, as beautiful as they may have been, had another purpose. After reclining on the board, the woman placed the flowers on her stomach at a point near the middle of the board. Her gown hung a foot (30 cm) or more below the board. As the magician began to talk, his assistant, who was behind a curtain, placed a steel rod into a hole in the board. The bouquet and gown provided a screen that prevented the audience from seeing the small gap in the curtain that occurred when the assistant connected the rod to the board. A mechanical device behind the screen enabled the assistant to raise and lower the board. In some cases, the device is so arranged that the board may be tipped as well as raised and lowered.

In a modified version of this illusion, the lady is covered with a sheet, elevated, and is found to have disappeared when the sheet is removed. As you might guess, the woman disappeared long before the sheet was removed. The table on which she lay sank down so that she could escape. The sheet rested on fine wires, invisible to the audience.

MIND READING • You hold a slip of paper against your forehead above the blindfold that covers your eyes. You are trying to determine the name of the U.S. president written on the paper. Finally, you say, "Harry Truman." Your assistant, who may be someone from the audience, takes the slip and sees that the name written on the slip is indeed Harry Truman.

Prior to doing this fabulous bit of mind reading, you ask members of the audience to name their favorite presidents. (You could ask for authors, movies, plays, or any other topic.) As people name presidents you write the names on a strip of paper, fold them up, and drop them into a hat. However, regardless of the name they say, you write "Harry Truman" on all the slips. To make it look good you might ask, "Let's see, Kennedy has two *n*'s, doesn't it?" Or, "How do you spell Eisenhower?"

After you've put all the slips in a hat, your assistant blindfolds you. A person from the audience draws a slip from the hat, opens it, reads it silently, and hands it to you. Then you do your amazing mind-reading feat. Meanwhile, your assistant has discarded all the other slips backstage.

Another mind-reading trick requires a good memory but no mind-reading ability. You ask people in the audience to write single-sentence messages on separate small sheets of paper. You then pass a hat among people in the audience asking them to drop their folded papers into the hat. At some point you stop to stir the papers. While your hand is in the hat, you grab one of the papers between your thumb and your palm so it is hidden from the audience. You then hand the hat to someone else and ask him or her to finish collecting the messages. You walk to the stage and stand with your back to the audience so you can't "peek." You open the paper and memorize the message.

When the hat is returned to the stage, you remove

one slip and hold it against your forehead. After pretending intense concentration, you repeat the message you read earlier with your back to the audience. Ask if anyone wrote that message. After the writer is identified, you open the slip and pretend to read the message you memorized. (Leaving out a word or two will help to make the process more believable.) Meanwhile, you memorize the message that was held against your forehead, the one that's on the paper you're looking at. These are the words you will read after you pick another slip from the hat and repeat the process.

The last slip you hold against your head must be the one you secretly removed when you handed the hat to someone else to pass among the audience. You can hold it hidden in your hand as you reach for what you announce will be your last reading. A nice final touch is to return each slip to the person who wrote it.

MENTAL TELEPATHY? • If you work with a partner, you can tell your audience that your long association together enables you to communicate with one another through mind waves. For example, you place nine cards on a table as shown in the photograph. You leave the room and a member of the audience chooses a card. Let's suppose he or she chooses the three of hearts. When you return, your partner will point to the king of diamonds as shown in the photograph and ask, "Is this the card?"

You respond, "No!" But you now know that the card chosen was the three of hearts because the position of your partner's finger when she points to the first card provided the signal. Notice that she points to the upper

Finger placement is the key to this card trick. The card serves as a "map" of all nine cards. Which card was chosen here?

right-hand corner of the card she touches. The cards form a rectangle. Because she pointed to the upper right-hand corner of the card, you know the three of hearts is the card that was chosen. Had the nine of spades been selected, your partner would have pointed to the center of the right-hand edge of the card. Had it been the ace of clubs, she would have pointed to the center of the card.

The initial card pointed to serves as a map of the nine cards that may be selected. If someone suspects signals, they may ask that the partner point first to the card selected. Consequently, the person who is to receive the "brain waves" must be ready to select the first card pointed to if that's what the signal indicates. For example, if the finger in the photo were at the same position on the three of hearts, then the signal indicates that card is the one selected.

A more complicated form of signals can be used to identify any object selected in a room. You suggest that with this more complicated communication, sound and an antenna are needed to create a signal that can be read. Vowels might be indicated with taps from a broom handle—your antenna. One tap indicates an A, two taps an E, three taps an I, etc. To communicate consonants you can use the first letter of sentences you utter as you go about the process of transferring mental signals. To throw your audience off the track, you can make all kinds of strange designs using the broom-handle antenna on a floor or carpet.

For example, to identify a lamp you could begin by saying, "Let's get going!"

The l in "Let's" indicates that the first letter of the object is l. Then tap the broom handle on the floor once to indicate the second letter is an a. Draw some strange figures on the floor with the broom handle to distract the audience as you say, "Maybe we should communicate more often."

By now your partner knows the first three letters are lam. All you have to do now is to start a final sentence with the letter p. You might say, "Perhaps we need a bigger antenna."

A MEMORY ILLUSION • Tell your audience that you have an uncanny knack for memorizing and that, in fact, you have memorized the numbers in the local telephone book. They won't believe you, of course, but you can prove to them that your memory is all that you claim.

Hand one member of your audience a telephone book. Present a second with a pad and paper. Ask the second person to write down any three-digit number such that all three digits are different. She might choose 672. Then ask her to reverse those digits (276) and subtract the smaller from the larger ($672 - 276 = 396$). Ask her if the remainder has three digits. If it doesn't, tell her to add a zero (for example 99 becomes 990). Next, tell her to reverse the order of the digits in the remainder (396 becomes 693). Add this to the number from which it came ($396 + 693 = 1089$).

Ask the person who has done the calculations to tell you the last two digits of the final number (1089). Have the first person turn to that page (89) in the telephone book. Then ask for the first two digits of the number (10). With your back to the audience, tell the first person to count down to the tenth name on page 89 of the book. He is then to write the number on a blackboard or in large print on a sheet of paper. Once the audience can see the number, you pretend to be struggling as you recite the same number that appears on the board or paper.

Now that you have convinced the audience of your amazing memory, take it one step further by announcing the name of the owner of that phone number. The person holding the phone book will confirm that you are again correct.

To do this trick, all you need do is memorize the tenth name and number on page 89 of the phone book. The mathematics are such that the answer will always be 1089. Can you explain why it will always be 1089?

AN ARITHMETIC ILLUSION • Tell a member of your audience that you can determine his birthday if he can do some simple arithmetic for you. Give him a piece of paper and a pencil and have him do the following:

Take the number of the month he was born. [Let's assume it's February (2).]

Multiply by 5. ($5 \times 2 = 10$.)

Add 4. ($10 + 4 = 14$.)

Multiply the sum by 10. ($14 \times 10 = 140$.)

Add 9. ($140 + 9 = 149$.)

Multiply that sum by 2. ($149 \times 2 = 298$.)

Add the number of the day of the month he was born. [Let's assume it's the 21st ($298 + 21 = 319$).]

Ask the subject for the number he has found (319 in this case). From this number subtract 100 and add 2 (in this case you get 221). The last two digits give the day of the month he was born. The first one or two give the month he was born.

Can you figure out how all this arithmetic enables you to find the person's birthday? Hint: what is the net effect of the multiplication and addition?

Now that you are able to use illusions to perform some "magic" tricks of your own, you should be able to better appreciate a show performed by a professional magician, mind reader, or illusionist. Knowing that what you see are illusions, you can concentrate on the skills that these performers use in deceiving their audiences.

FOR FURTHER READING

Beeler, Nelson F., and Franklyn M. Branley. *Experiments in Optical Illusions.* New York: Crowell, 1951.

Gardner, Martin. *Entertaining Science Experiments with Everyday Objects.* New York: Dover, 1981.

Gregory, Richard L. *The Intelligent Eye.* New York: McGraw-Hill, 1970.

———. *Eye and Brain: The Psychology of Seeing.* New York: McGraw-Hill, 1971.

Henning, Fritz. *Concept and Composition.* Cincinnati: North Light Publishers, 1983.

Luckiesh, M. *Visual Illusions: Their Causes, Characteristics, and Applications.* New York: Dover, 1965.

Meyer, Jerome S. *Boiling Water in a Paper Cup and Other Unbelievables.* New York: Scholastic, 1970.

Minnaert, M. *The Nature of Light and Color in the Open Air.* New York: Dover, 1954.

Ulrey, Lloyd K. *Magnificent Illusions.* Oxnard, California: Psychic Books, 1987.

Wertenbaker, Lael, and the Editors of U.S. News Books. *The Eye: Window to the World.* Washington, D.C.: U.S. News Books, 1981.

White, Laurence B., Jr., and Ray Broekel. *Optical Illusions.* New York: Franklin Watts, 1986.

Numerous articles in the magazines *Scientific American* and *Psychology Today* are also good sources of information about illusions and experiments related to illusions.

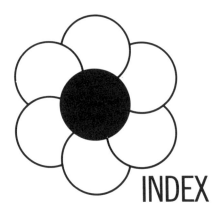

INDEX

Page numbers in *italics*
refer to illustrations.

Judd illusion, 53, 54

Kanizsa, Gaetano, 59
Kanizsa triangle, 59–61
Kaufman, Lloyd, 96
Kennedy, John M., 61–63
Kuffler, Stephen, 28

Land, Edwin, 31, 32, 36, 46
Lateral enhancement, 99–100
Lateral inhibition, 28–29, 55, 56, 99–100
Learning, effect on perception of objects, 16
Lenses, 23–24, 44
Light, 10, 17; absorption of, 83–84; and after-images, 43; cells used for vision, 25–26; color after passing through haze, 67; diffusion of, 91; diverging of, 89; effect on a cat eye, 28; emitted by photopores, 21; intensity affecting signals to brain, 80; path at sunset and midday, 83–84, 85, 86, *87;* reflection of, 91, *93,* 94; refraction, 85–90, *88;* refraction and reflection in raindrops, 22–23; spread into a spectrum, 89–90
Light box, 32–33
Lines: curvature, 17; in op art, 18; length, 17; straight, 48
Looming, 89

Mach bands, 29, 94–95
Magicians' tricks, 17, 19, 104; birthday determination, 116–117; disappearing woman, 109–110; floating lady, 109; mental telepathy, 112–115, *113;* mind reading, 110–112; mirrors used, 106–109; phone-number memory, 115–116; playing-card mapping, 112–115, *113;* rabbits, 105; ribbons, 105; sawing people, 105–106; sleight-of-hand, 104, 105